C.1

Lives That Inspire

Lives That Inspire

by Beatrice Plumb

Author of—
Here's for a Good Time
The Master Banquet and Party Book
Wedding Anniversary Celebrations

Publishers
T. S. DENISON & COMPANY, INC.
Minneapolis

Contents

Foreword

When I was a little girl, I especially liked to be with certain people, because, as I explained to my parents, they made me "want to be good."

As I grew older, I was drawn to others for the same reason.

When I began writing stories, I sent my first manuscript to "Christian Herald," because it contained articles, stories, and poems that made me want to be good.

In the years that followed, I wrote chiefly about men and women whose lives inspired me, and so I hoped would inspire others.

As the articles appeared, I pasted them into a big scrapbook, now getting worn and shabby.

Last year, the thought came to me, "I should get rid of all these scrapbooks. They take up too much room"; but before doing so, I re-read some of the articles I had written about people who had done—or were still doing—great things for others. Just reading them made me want to be good!

Then I thought, "Why not pick out a few and print them in a book?" And here it is!

I pray as I put this small offering into the Lord's multiplying hand that He will bless it, and use it to perform some miracle to His glory.

Acknowledgments

An immensely great acknowledgment is made to the following, without whose assistance there could have been no book:

Abingdon Press for permission to reprint most of the poems quoted in the Jane Merchant chapter.

Christian Herald for permission to reprint eleven of my articles which now appear as chapters in this book.

Harper & Brothers for permission to reprint my booklet, "Grace Noll Crowell, the Poet and the Woman."

Together Magazine for permission to reprint "Jane Merchant: Poetess of Faith"; and to the following for permission to reprint poems, or lines from poems in the same: David C. Cook Publishing Co., Curtis Publishing Co., Progressive Farmer, Saturday Evening Post, and These Times.

The Atlanta Journal, Georgia, for thermofax copy of the 1961 interview of Sergeant York by Andrew Sparks for the Sunday Magazine.

Bud Guest, WJR, Detroit, Michigan, for helpful material about his father, Eddie Guest.

The Detroit News, for information about the Nancy Brown Peace Carillon.

Also to the authors of the following books—veritable gold mines to the seeking author, digging for nuggets of dates and facts.

Edgar A. Guest, a Biography, by Royce Howes
The Little Professor of Piney Woods, by Beth Day
Miracle in Mississippi, by Leslie Harper Purcell

Introduction

Beatrice Plumb is the favorite person as well as the favorite author of a multitude of readers — and worthily so. She writes always to the heart but equally to the minds of the young and older. In this, her latest volume, she has brought together the most helpful and popular of her articles. Some of these remain as household favorites across America—and beyond. Millions read or saw "The Little Professor of Piney Woods" which was reprinted many times and used on the "Voice of America." Without doubt Beatrice Plumb's articles played their part in getting "The Little Professor" on the TV program "This Is Your Life," which resulted in the raising of more than seven hundred thousand dollars for that not so little "Hero's" school in the deep South.

"Just Eddie" was a poignant tribute to Edgar A. Guest, which is now merged with "This Is All I Counted Splendid" with added material supplied by "Bud," the immortal Eddie's son. "I Belong to the King" was written about Ida L. Reed, the backwoods hymn-writer who was a Grace Noll Crowell of an earlier day. But here again there is added material with the recital of a dedicated woman's heroic struggles against illness and poverty.

Lives That Inspire moves off the beaten path and, traveling a trail that leads to the hearts of us all, tells the story of those who in every walk of life and down at the very grass roots of life itself have made their lives meaningful. Here is a businessman who gives away thousands and tens of thousands of copies of Warner Sallman's Head of Christ and does so as a practical plan to inspire these thousands to remember Christ in their daily lives.

The author's deeply moving story of Sergeant York, who was named by Marshal Foch as having done "the greatest thing accomplished by any private soldier of all the armies of Europe," points up the fact that this "Tennessee hillbilly" had been a devout conscientious pacifist who had asked God to show him how to be a conscientious objector with a clear conscience! That was his first prayer. But God told him to go and so he went. And now his name was headlined in the war news of Europe and America. Beatrice Plumb gives in detail the story of what this simple and devout mountaineer did, and of course she tells us much more. One of his sons, Edward, named for York's Italian commander, is a Nazarene preacher. What a chapter this is.

Grace Noll Crowell is one of the most widely known and best loved personalities in the field of American literature. She has a worthy place in this delightful volume. There are intimate details added to her story. Even those of us who have known Mrs. Crowell for many years had not discovered them and we are grateful to the author who has now given them to us.

Miss Plumb pays her grateful tribute to a Sunday School teacher in England who came to her when she was a little girl of thirteen and sadly adrift with the sudden death of her mother. She calls this "My Star in the East."

For me, one of the most moving of the chapters is the story of Willie Lee Buffington, the "po' white millhand," who built a little string of log-cabin libraries for destitute Negroes. This is the merging of three of her previously published articles, "Joy-bells Ringing," "The Brotherhood of Books," and "He Works the Miracle." But every chapter of the volume is a spiritual experience for the reader.

Beatrice Plumb proves with her radiant pen that life does not begin at forty, as once was written, but that it does or may begin for you here and now and where you are.

—Dr. Daniel A. Poling

Lives That Inspire

A Dream, a Dime—and Faith

This is the story of Willie Lee Buffington, the young white mill hand of Edgefield, South Carolina, who, "with a dream and a dime," set out in the depths of the Big Depression to beg for his poor Negro neighbors. For bread? No, for books!

As a result of his efforts, carried on to this day, there are now more than a million books, housed in over a hundred little libraries, dotted through the rural districts and small towns of South Carolina and Georgia.

Six of these small libraries are housed in rustic little log cabins; several in buildings of stone, cement blocks, or shingles; and others in rooms especially provided for them in book-hungry Negro schools.

Each link in this unique chain, known as "Faith Cabin Library," has from two thousand to ten thousand books, and all are in sections of the country where, but for him, there would be no such library.

Back of all this is his grandmother's Bible. And

her teaching that "a little bit, blessed by the Lord, goes a long way."

Willie Lee was a little lad then. His mother had died when he was two, and his father had brought him to his Granny's cabin in the cotton, to be cared for. All about them in the pines sagged the shacks of the backwoods settlement, densely populated with Negroes, eking out a bare existence.

Granny had little education, but enough to read her Bible aloud to the little lad at her knee. And when the light waned, she could read on from memory, or tell him stories about the little boys in the Bible.

Need was all around her. Perhaps that is why she liked to tell how Jesus wanted the hungry multitude fed, and how He said to His disciples, "Give ye them to eat."

"You can be starved for other things beside bread, Willie Lee," explained Granny, "such as a chance to be somebody . . . or school learnin' . . . or a book to read."

The little lad, with a fluff of almost white hair—they called him "Cotton Top"—would listen, his eyes big with the wonder of it, as she went on to tell the rest of the story; how a boy in the crowd by the Sea of Galilee gave his lunch to the Lord. Just his lunch! But it was enough. It fed the multitude.

"All you need do, Willie Lee," she told him, "is to put the little bit you have in the Lord's hand. HE works the miracle."

A few years later, when his father married again,

Willie Lee went home, to trudge his daily three miles
to the two-room schoolhouse in the woods, and to play
with the Negro boys whose fathers worked in the
cotton.

He was a nine-year-old boy in ragged overalls,
when he formed his first real friendship—an odd, deep
comradeship, destined to shape his whole life, and
inspire his book ministry.

He stood wailing beside his home because a heedless foot had ruined his mud pie. Presently, a passer-by
paused beside him. The boy looked up through discon-
solate tears into the kindly, lined face of an old Negro
schoolteacher — Professor Simpkins to his pupils,
"Uncle Eury" to his white neighbors.

"Be a man," the gentle Negro admonished the
weeping white lad. "The world needs men."

When Uncle Eury walked on, "Cotton Top," inspired by something, he knew not what, walked alongside. He listened and learned.

Being a man, to Uncle Eury, meant living right;
taking the hardships without a whimper; striving for
a good education; dedicating it to the service of others.

Little did the mud-smeared youngster know that
one day that word "Others" would become his life's
motto, to be hung on the wall of every new Faith
Cabin Library!

Willie Lee was already learning "the Three R's"
in the schoolhouse in the woods. Now he began studying to live right. He went regularly to Sunday school

where his dad was superintendent. He dared to dream
of one day being a minister.

But by the time he had reached the top of his cotton patch school, he was needed at home, for now
there were five little sisters there. His school days,
they told him, were over. And so, too, almost at once,
were his farming days, for with the coming of the boll
weevil to South Carolina in 1920, came ruin. The Buf-
fingtons lost their farm.

Dad and twelve-year-old Willie Lee found work
in the sawmill. Together, they made two-fifty a day.
For five years they followed the mill from one plan-
tation to another. During that time, the lad's only
touch with school was the books he borrowed from the
few Uncle Eury owned.

Then, from the very sawdust of his daily job, came
his chance! He heard of a school in Georgia where a
poor boy could go and work his way, earn his learning.

"If you want to go, son," said his dad, "I'll spare
you . . . somehow."

"I want you to go to high school," urged Uncle
Eury, "to college, to divinity school. I want you to be
a preacher of the Gospel."

Two months later, Willie Lee trudged through the
Gate of Opportunity of the famous Martha Berry
School, near Rome, Georgia. Three hundred miles from
home, with exactly $2.80 to his name—a backwoods
boy, with a longing to learn.

Within a few hours of his arrival, he was literally
digging for an education, for his first job was spading

up a sewer. Later, he was promoted to driving the trash wagon.

Trash? Treasure to him! For among the library litter was precious reading matter—old magazines, clippings, publicity brochures. Hungrily, he picked them out of the rubbish, took them home with him to paste into a home-made scrapbook. Now he had something to send to Uncle Eury!

A matron, making a routine check of the boys' rooms, came across that book of salvaged trash. News of it reached official ears. Willie Lee was called to the office, and, to his incredulous joy, was told that he had been assigned to two days' work a week in the school library.

Oh, happy day! Then, indeed, did new worlds open up before his amazed young eyes. The wisdom of the ages between the covers of a book! Oh, if only his friends back home could share in all this—especially Uncle Eury!

For every month he received a letter from his faithful old colored friend, bringing news of the home settlement, the same gentle admonition to "be a man" —and frequently a dollar bill from his meager salary of forty dollars. Rich gift of the poor to the poor!

"Some day," vowed Willie Lee, "I'll pay it all back ... pass it on ... you'll see—"

The following year, instead of going home for the summer, Willie Lee stayed at the school to work, in order to accumulate enough credits to pay for future schooling. Under the strain, his health broke.

"Go home, and rest," the school doctor advised him. But when he reached his native backwoods, he found his father battling the depression, struggling to support his family. Willie Lee, now nineteen, turned in to help, working in the textile mill at Edgefield, South Carolina.

"And now," he sighs, "a loom was my altar." Before it, he silently poured out all his lost hope of a good education — "for others"; of helping his poor Negro friends; of one day being a minister of the Gospel. It seemed as if some heedless heel had crushed out all his dreams, just as it had the mud castle of his little-boy days.

Then again there seemed to come to him that gentle admonition, "Be a man! The world needs men."

Poor old Uncle Eury! So proud of the new Rosenwald school he had worked so hard to get; of its three rooms with modern desks and blackboards. But, the distressed Willie Lee had noticed, with not a single book. Not even a shelf to put them on!

"The Lord will provide," the patient old professor had assured him. "I have faith. The books will come."

But *how?* Willie Lee wrestled with the problem as he trudged home from a visit to the new school, just before its dedication. He remembered those precious dollar bills, the cheery letters, that had come to him when he was a struggling, homesick working-student at the Berry School. If only now he could repay Uncle Eury by giving him books for his new school! But, with the mills now operating only two days a week, he had no money.

As he plodded on, he thought wistfully of the well-filled shelves of the Berry School library. Suddenly, in a revealing flash, he recalled that many of those books had not been purchased by the school. They had been good used books—donated!

And now it was his Granny's voice that seemed to come to him from that cabin of his little boyhood. "All you need do, Willie Lee, is put the little bit you have in the Lord's hand. HE works the miracle!"

He put his hand in his pocket, found his last dime. With it, he bought five two-cent stamps. Back home, he chose at random from his old Sunday school quarterlies, the names of five people who might have a book to spare. Then he wrote to each a letter, reading in part: "The Negroes here have no books. Good books will help them more than anything else. I want to start a library for them. Could you send me a book for it? Or if you have none to spare, then please give a stamp so that I can write to someone else."

For two months, he waited in vain for a reply. No books, no stamps! Then came an airmail letter from a kind minister in New York City, saying that he had read Willie Lee's appeal to his congregation, and some books were on the way.

A little later they came, freight-prepaid. ONE THOUSAND of them! Young Buffington could hardly believe his eyes. He had asked for five books — and here was a library! God had made the miracle!

After grateful Uncle Eury had made his selection, Buffington's joy was dimmed by consternation. Where was there a safe place to house the wealth of books that remained? He called for helpers to assist him in carting them to a little local church. Here they stacked them around the altar, and called a community meeting to discuss the problem.

"These books are all yours," he announced to his astonished audience. "How about building a library to put them in?"

Thus began the making of the first link in that remarkable add-a-library chain. Under Uncle Eury's competent supervision, they began building a pine-pole log cabin, 18 by 22 feet, with a large open fireplace, and a natural rock chimney.

Some of the logs were donated by generous white land owners; others were cut from the school land; still others were given or pledged by local Negroes. Surplus lumber was used to pay for other building needs. Nimble black fingers padded the barrel chairs, covered them with bright cretonne. A colored friend donated a broken piano for a library table; a white friend, a battery radio. Big, black hands gently arranged the books on the shelves, and the magazines— many old, few new—on the piano-table. On the wall, young Buffington hung a motto, bearing the one word, "Others."

An old Negro woman who, at that time, could neither read nor write, gave the little log structure its name. Looking at it with admiring eyes, she said, "It was built by faith. Let's call it 'Faith Cabin Library.'"

It was dedicated in December, 1932, by young Buffington, "to the glory of God and the uplift of mankind." He ended his address by words he did not then know were prophetic, "May your influence spread far beyond these four walls!"

He appointed Uncle Eury as librarian of the new little library. Then he went home satisfied. He had paid back some of his debt to his old friend.

The happy ending? No, the blessed beginning! News of this young Southerner's extraordinary concern for his Negro neighbors caught the imagination of educators, librarians, social workers, and columnists. One of the latter, after an enlightening visit to Faith Cabin Library, went home to tell his readers the front page news of demonstrated good will; to mention Buffington's name and that of Julius Rosenwald in the same sentence!

"The part that Rosenwald played in the educational advancement of the Negro race," he wrote, "is an epic in modern life, in racial history; and yet his work is not so significant and outstanding as that of this Edgefield mill operator."

Rosenwald, he pointed out, had millions of dollars; Buffington, one thin dime. Rosenwald saw the Southern Negro through a long perspective, whereas Buffington rubbed elbows with him in a mill village where the black man outnumbered the white, where Caucasian and Negro were in direct competition, and where feeling often ran high.

"There is a vast difference," commented this Southern sage, "in looking at the racial problem from a distance of a thousand miles, and looking at it from a distance of a hundred yards. That's what makes the achievement of this man the more startling."

All of which puzzled young Buffington. "Black . . . white . . . we're all God's children," he says, simply, as if that should solve any problem.

The mill hand's neighborly project had become news. Editorials were written about it and by-lined columns. More and more books poured in. Soon there were four little cabin libraries in the cotton.

But now Buffington began to feel the pressure of the work involved — pressure that was to mount in the ensuing years — for with the National Recovery Act, in 1933, his working hours were reduced from eleven hours a day to eight, and he had seized the chance to go back to high school.

He was now a 25-year-old married man, with a family. He attended school from eight until noon, then changed his clothes and reported for another day's work at the mill. Then study until bedtime, after which, while all but the breadwinner were sound asleep, he worked until dawn, acknowledging books, answering mail, attending to his library mission.

It was a gruelling struggle, yet in the next ten years, he completed his high school work, and entered Furman University to prepare for the ministry. Three years later, with an A.B. degree, he entered Crozer Theological School at Chester, Pennsylvania, won a Bachelor of Divinity degree, and finally reached his goal with a Master's degree from the University of Pennsylvania.

What a day that was for Uncle Eury! For not only did he see his dreams for his white friend realized, but he, himself, received an honorary A.B. degree, designating, in his case, "a benefactor."

During all these busy, anxious years, Buffington continued his library work. While he was at Furman, seven new libraries were established; while he was at Crozer, six. And on his desk — and on his heart — were pleas for a dozen more.

There were times when the burden seemed more than he could carry. While he was at Crozer, he wrote to a friend, "This is the fifth year now that Mrs. Buffington and I have lived on a margin of existence. I sometimes wonder if I should not give less attention to this library work and try to get a small church while I am in the Seminary. But I *know* that this mission is serving a wider field and a greater number than I could possibly serve as a pastor. The idea occurs to me in times of crisis — when the gas and light bills come due, and there are no funds . . . It is the acid test of one's religion to sometimes hold on to an ideal where it seemingly doesn't pay."

He held on! And so the chain of useful little libraries grew ever longer, as one writer after another told of this brotherhood of books, in *Christian Herald, Lutheran Standard, Sunday Digest, American Magazine, Saturday Evening Post, Kiwanis Magazine, Coronet,* and *Guideposts.* Just three-and-a-half inches of print in the last-named, brought in enough books to establish another library.

And what a brotherhood it was — and is! After

reading an article about Faith Cabin Library in *The Christian Herald*, in 1935—there were only four log cabin libraries then—the Rev. Caspar Garrigues, president of the Ministerial Association in Iowa City, Iowa, launched a city-wide campaign to collect books for the cabins in the cotton, with the following denominational churches, and clubs and libraries cooperating: Baptist, Catholic, Christian, Congregational, Episcopal, Jewish, Lutheran, Mennonite, Methodist, Unitarian, Presbyterian, School of Religion of the State University, Altrusa Club, Iowa Women's Club, Iowa City Public Library, the University Library—and the community at large!

"That's his peculiar genius," said a minister, of Buffington, "erasing not only race, but denominational lines."

The goal of 2,000 books was reached—and passed. Then reached, and passed again . . . and still again. Even after their shipment of 6,000 books and 1,500 magazines had reached the backwoods, the enthusiasm of that midwestern city went right on sizzling. So the special committee became a permanent one, to continue to send books regularly "to fill the gaps" on the shelves of their library, located at Bettis Academy, Trenton, South Carolina — a high school and junior college, with a grade school also on the campus.

There is the glory of a miracle about each link of the chain. Inside each library is some spiritual bond of fellowship, as if each volume comes wrapped in an invisible cover, all aglow with the spirit that pervaded those who collected the books. And this, regardless of whether a great college garnered its hundreds of "very excellent textbooks," or one lone, disabled veteran canvassed several counties to bring in his two tons of less-learned volumes.

The Methodist women have been Buffington's staunchest friends. They have sent in books by the thousands, providing enough for at least fifteen libraries.

And, most wonderful of all, they helped to give him his heart's desire, by making it financially possible for him to devote most of his time to his book ministry.

In 1951, The Board of Trustees of Paine College, Augusta, Georgia, made the Faith Cabin Library an official extension of the College! It is supported by the Division of National Missions of the Methodist Church and The Woman's Division of Christian Service of The Methodist Church. These agencies supply the Rev. Buffington's salary as Director of Faith Cabin Library, as well as the allowance for postage and travel.

However, he is still Professor of Sociology at the College, and is chairman of the Committee on Religious Life and Work, which is responsible for Sunday Vespers, the College Christian Fellowship and all other religious activities, such as Sunday School, YM, YW, and the Ministerial Union, which is made up of pre-ministerial students.

In November, 1958, the Rev. W. L. Buffington was presented with the tenth annual Lane Bryant Award of One Thousand Dollars for the individual "making the largest contribution to the American community and the American family."

Did his thoughts go back twenty years, to when, as he entered Crozer, he received the first big gift of his life—a second-hand car (and how he needed it, with some of his libraries a hundred miles away!) from the congregations of the First Lutheran, and the Baptist churches of Norwich, Connecticut?

"It has practically new tires," the excited collegian wrote to a friend; then, as the missionary in him asserted itself, he added, "I accepted it only because it could be used to help others and Faith Cabin Library, which, in turn, serves others."

And Uncle Eury? He did not live long after he had seen his "Cotton Top" receive his Master's degree, and lies buried beside the first little Faith Cabin Library, as he wished.

Tithed Tuition

I had long wanted to meet Ben T. Largen, the man who tithes young people into college, founder of an organization that holds out a friendly hand — with cash in it! — to worthy youngsters to whom a higher education would be but a dream, but for Tithers, Incorporated.

Today I met him. And I want you to meet him, too. As I watched him come up my garden path, a six-footer in a gray suit, I thought he looked rather like a football player, or a farmer turned businessman.

I guessed right. He was born on a Tennessee farm, worked his way through Morgan's Prep School, then went to Georgia Tech on a football scholarship. Later, turning to business, he was for seventeen years in charge of the real estate department of the F. W. Woolworth Company for the entire Southeast, and now is in the real estate business in Coral Gables, Florida.

As he settled into a comfortable chair on my porch, I took a good look at this big fellow who has the South in his voice and manner, and about him the deep, quiet happiness of those who put God first.

"There's nothing unusual in what we're doing," he began in his practical way. "There could be Tithers, Incorporated, in every state of the Union. It's a flexible plan. It can be modified or adapted, followed by an individual or a group, formally or informally. All it needs is a small start—and it grows."

He started small. He was just one lone tither, helping two bright little orphan girls who had nothing toward a higher education but a longing for it.

That was in 1946. Since then, Tithers, Inc., has helped 196 young people to a higher education.

"What gave you the idea, in the first place?" I asked him.

Well, he explained, it had all started with his tithing. In the fall of 1945, he and his wife made a pledge that starting the first of January, they would tithe their income. No, it wasn't a New Year's resolution. At the time he had a job that paid his salary once a year. He knew he would get a sizable check, and figured it would give him a nice tithe to distribute.

After he had given to his church and the other usual good causes, there was still some of "the Lord's money" in the bank. He wanted to use it where it would pay dividends for the Kingdom. What should he do with it?

"It suddenly came to me," said Mr. Largen, "that I could use the extra money to help some boy or girl—maybe an orphan—get an education. But where could

I find one? Then I remembered the Children's Home at Decatur, and got in touch with the superintendent. He had in his care, at that time, two orphan girls who were ready and eager for college."

"And that's how Tithers, Incorporated, started," I finished for him.

"No," he said, "then it was purely a personal matter. That is all I ever intended it to be—just my own little plan for using a part of my tithe."

It might have stayed that way, had it not been for the young adults of College Park Methodist Church, near Atlanta, Georgia. They were looking for a speaker for their evening meeting. Would Mr. Largen give a talk on tithing?

Gladly! That was his favorite topic. It still is. As part of the talk, he told them of the thrill he was getting out of "tithing" the orphans to college. When the speech was over, the young people crowded about him, to thank him. There were four who wanted to do more.

"We tithe," they told him. "Can't we help by adding part of our tithes to yours? Then, perhaps, you can give four scholarships next year."

That quickly, the project got gloriously out of hand! An organization seemed logical. They met in the church to form one. There were twelve charter members. Thus Tithers, Incorporated, was born.

"When they came in to help, and others like them," said Mr. Largen, "it became possible to send eight students to college, and then more and more, until today there are 36 boys and girls in college, under this program—on a budget of $9,639!"

I stared at that low figure. How could they do so much on so little?

Because, I learned, all concerned help. It is no charity, but a willing pooling of all resources. The student and his family contribute whatever they can. The college helps by granting a student-aid job, or scholarship; often both. Then Tithers, Incorporated, gives a cash scholarship, averaging $250, to assure the student a full year at the college of his choice. That supplies the important psychological push. And every first of September, Tithers, Inc., starts raising funds to return these students to college, and to add as many more as funds will permit.

"How do you locate students who need help?" I asked. He laughed at that. "They locate us!" he assured me. "A bright student from an accredited high school may be eligible for several scholarships offered by colleges, yet not have the necessary money to avail himself of any. In which case, recommended by school president or college president, he applies for a Tithers scholarship. We get many of our applicants from the colleges from which our former tithe-students were graduated. Of course, we always get more requests than we can grant."

Surprisingly enough, I learned that donations come from some who are not tithers! From those who never had a child to educate; from parents who lost a daughter while she was still in school; as memorials to dead soldier-sons; and from those who, in their youth, longed in vain for a college education.

I had a touchy question to ask. Did this form of tithing take from the church plate? To which Tither Largen gives a forthright "No." For when they needed a membership pledge card, they asked Bishop Arthur J. Moore to help them word it. In part, it reads: "It is understood that my contribution to Tithers, Incorporated, will not affect or diminish my contribution to my church."

"That's how we all wanted it to read," said Mr. Largen. "The church must come first."

Every year, his organization issues a brochure, showing the pictures of the new crop of tithe-students who have been awarded scholarships. Mr. Largen drew my attention to a quotation on the cover of one of them. "That's our chief aim," he said, with a deep earnestness, and read aloud Daniel Webster's wise words, "Who gives to his country an educated Christian serves God and man forever."

Then, as we looked at the rows of pretty or handsome, alert young faces in the various brochures, he pointed out one youngster after another, who was on the way to becoming — or had already become — an educated Christian.

"Just look at this lad's nice, lop-sided grin!" I laughed.

"That," said Mr. Largen, "is one of the three Kay brothers. We were able to help all of them answer the call to the ministry."

Their parents were living, but with a large family, there was no money for college. "We had very little to go on," their wonderful mother informed me later. "We've given them food and clothing, and put them through high school. I have tried to teach them to aim high."

Of her children, taught "to aim high," Lulu was then a Home Mission worker for the Presbyterian Church; Jean, a registered nurse; John and Terry, preparing for the ministry; and Tooms Kay, Jr., was the 26-year-old minister of a 254-year-old church, set in the midst of the busy county of Queens, in the city of New York.

His two former churches had been small ones, rural and suburban. And now, at last, he had this historic city church to challenge his strength and soul.

In a letter to Mr. Largen, he wrote, "As I face expectant congregations, I have the feeling that this is the day for which God permitted me to be born. Yet, upon reflection, I know that God's will is done only as people incline themselves to do it. Those people who gave money to Tithers, Inc., years ago, helped shape my destiny in a way they will never know. So I not only thank God for my ministry, but I also thank Him for those many unknown and unnamed people who went the second mile, so that I could answer His call."

There were girls, too, who paid rich dividends in Christian character and service. Grace Hadaway Boswell, for instance, who, at that time, had a full-time teaching position at the University of Georgia. Grace's father died when she was five years old, leaving her mother with five children to support. Grace dropped out of high school to help at home until she found that by working nights, she could help and still attend school.

Three years of this could not kill Grace's longing to be a teacher. She had managed to save a little money from her night jobs, and with this, a scholarship and a part-time job she dared to aspire to one year at Reinhardt Junior College. Two years later, she was first-honor student of her class, and was urged to go on to senior college. How could she, with no money?

Tithers, Inc., offered her the friendly hand, with cash in it. LaGrange College granted her a scholarship and a part-time job for two years—and Grace was on her way up the academic ladder. Later, she won a $2,400 Alumni Foundation Fellowship to work toward a Ph.D. degree in English.

Grace wrote to Mr. Largen, "Can I ever express my gratitude? May my life manifest it!"

It does. For with Grace, education and religion go hand-in-hand. Who can measure the influence of this lovely young woman, good as she is brilliant, as she gives knowledge, guidance and inspiration to hundreds of young people!

It is records such as these that gladden the heart of Ben T. Largen, who found it no easy thing to continue his tithing in the years when his salary was "not too large," as he puts it, and he had two daughters of his own in college.

Although founded by a Methodist layman, and its original trustees were all Methodists, Tithers, Incorporated, is nonsectarian in its benefits, and has issued scholarships to boys and girls of many denominations.

Mr. Largen, now in real estate in Coral Gables, Florida, is still closely affiliated with the organization. He is a member of the Coral Gables Methodist Church, where he is a member of the official board, and teacher of an adult class.

A Jewel of a Juel

"You have multiple sclerosis," the grave-eyed doctor told her, "go home and give everything up. Prepare to be completely paralyzed in a year's time."

Juel Reed Cover, described by her publisher as a "whizz" of a newspaper woman, flinched at the foreboding prognosis. She knew much about this baffling disease of the central nervous system that strikes the young adult— rarely children or oldsters—and which has defied all efforts of research to find its cause or cure.

But go home and give up? The spunky, red-headed newspaper woman had just one word to say to that— a stubborn "No!"

She went right on newspapering, bowling, swimming, golfing. She admits that a slowing down crept up on her, but almost imperceptibly.

In 1953, an exacerbation—the medical term for an acute stage of the dread disease—hit her suddenly, bringing complete paralysis. After weeks of hospitalization, she returned to work, on crutches.

There could be no more bowling — she was an expert at it—and no more after-work golfing with her husband. But she learned to walk unaided, and continued her newspaper work.

Four years later, the second exacerbation hit; and this time she left the hospital in a walker. "Couldn't use crutches," she explains, breezily, "I was such a clumsy cow, I kept stepping on my own feet, and falling down." But she went back to work.

"Every day," she recalls, with a chuckle, "my walker was thrown down the steps, while I crawled down via clothesline, and then it zipped along with me to the office; then out on covering assignments to which I could drive close."

In 1959, the third exacerbation hit, and a summer hospital stay left her in a wheelchair.

She was advised to give up her strenuous job. But not Juel. There was no room in the already bulging news office for a wheelchair. What matter? She lived only a few blocks away from it. A branch news room could be transferred to her home. A copy boy could run stories over to the Daily News office as fast as she could type them, and she could cover her beat by phone.

Thus Juel Reed Cover carried on as editor of *The Daily News*, Port Clinton, Ohio—the state's only woman editor of a daily newspaper. Covering a beat that includes sheriff, courthouse, churches, schools, society, municipal court, Coast Guard, highway patrol, police, plus a sprinkling of sports, features, and her well-known daily column.

She received many newspaper awards. In 1960, she was named one of the ten Toledo, Ohio women to win the Blade's distinguished citizenship award.

But it is what she is doing in her limited spare time that makes her a truly great woman. It really started in 1955, when she received a call from a Chicago TV program, asking her to appear on the show. They had been told about her by a viewer who thought such an actively working multiple sclerosis victim was news.

As a result of the telecast, Juel received letters from MS patients, from all over the nation. After the first flurry, there remained a core of regular correspondents who found that it helped immensely to write to this cheery, courageous pen-pal who was one of them, and so could fully understand their plight; someone with whom they could compare notes, and exchange experiences.

Most of them had been left paralyzed, either partially or completely. Some had not left their home for years; some got out with the aid of crutches, walkers, and braces. Some were plucky and fighting; others had given up in despair.

Juel's heart went out to all of them, but especially to the completely paralyzed. One such victim was "Budd" Hegele, with whom she had been corresponding since the telecast. She marveled at his lively, amusing letters, which he dictated to his wife. Here was a young man, a former teacher, trapped physically, whose agile mind darted about in a dozen different fields — world affairs, politics, sports, music — who, although he had his blue moments, refused to let this disabling disease shrink his world. She wished her other MS-ers could get the lift of such letters.

When her dear friends, Darrell and Helen Fadely moved near to where Budd lived, she asked them to call on him. She knew the Hegeles only by letter, but she knew instinctively that they and the Fadelys were akin in spirit.

That was a blessed call for hundreds of MS-ers! For Helen and Budd put their creative heads together, and conceived the novel idea of bringing out a manuscript magazine, written by MS-ers for MS-ers — "a book of letters," a Round Robin. Those who contributed letters were to be known as "robins"; each issue, a "flight"; new members, "fledgings"; and Helen's home town, Salem, where the magazine would be published, "the nest."

As a start, they asked the multiple sclerosis victims who had been writing to Juel to now write to Helen. Then she typed their letters, assembled them as a magazine, added some of her own cute drawings, and a gay, seasonal cover, and mailed a copy to every letter writer.

Thus *The Round Robin* was born, with Juel Reed Cover as supervisory editor; Helen L. Fadely as Salem editor, and Budd as consultant and regular contributor.

The first issue, published around Thanksgiving, 1956, with a chirpy robin on the cover, contained only seven letters, and only a dozen copies were issued.

But soon the "robins" came flocking, as one MS-er told another, and each issue of the unique little magazine chirped with more ideas of how to help one another; how to come to terms with problems the disease creates; how to "keep on keeping on."

As issue followed issue, letters came from all sorts and conditions of victims — from a doctor, registered nurse, editor, teacher, newspaper man, athlete, pilot, policeman, mechanic, saleslady, script writer, factory worker, veteran of two world wars, commercial photographer.

Today, over 200 free copies of a much-enlarged *Round Robin* go out to MS-ers in Ohio, Michigan, Texas, Mexico, Arkansas, New York, Pennsylvania, and even to England and Scotland.

The work of making the magazine is now shared by willing hands, several of them those of MS victims. Betty, in spite of being in a wheel chair and suffering from serious tremors, types great batches of pages for the *Robin's* multigraphing machines. The Y-Teeners do the art covers, and members of the local chapter of the National Secretarial Association, of which Helen is a member, come in two evenings a week, for every issue, and on six machines type the bulk of the incoming letters—many of which have been painfully written, a few lines at a time, by crippled hands.

Church and civic groups help. The Salem Kiwanis Club pay all production costs. "All one has to do," says Helen, "is show the need. Nothing is so contagious as kindness."

Each issue starts with a letter from Juel—as informal as a chat over her garden hedge, alive with her characteristic gaiety, grit, gumption, and often delightful goofiness; but always with some such bracing message, as: "There are a lot of things worse than a physical handicap. A crippled spirit, for instance. As long as our spirits are free and soaring, what do wheel chairs and the like mean? MS can hold us down, physically—but the sky's the limit, otherwise."

Next comes a letter from the Salem editor, Helen, aglow with ideas for ways to enlarge the MS-ers' world, and with plans that give them a feeling of being useful — and needed.

Then come the "Robins'" letters, arranged by states, for easy reference. The writers tell what has happened to them since they last wrote; of new treatments they are receiving; funny family incidents; their trials and triumphs; their occasional outings. An Ohio humorist, an MS-er who is still able to do a daily column for his newspaper, contributes welcome laughs. Another victim, a nurse, gives medical counsel in lay language. One sends clippings, telling of the success of other handicapped persons, or helpful quotations, as: "When Heaven permits a heavy burden to be put upon you, there will always be an arm to support you."

All through the magazine are clever drawings — Helen once taught art — often amusing take-offs of some news item in a Robin's letter. Thus, a featherless robin heads the letter of one who had just returned from a strenuous bout in the hospital, and who wrote, "They sure took the feathers off me!"

Every issue has a special theme, tied to the season's

main activity, or a red-letter day in the month. One February issue was hailed with shouts of delight by every MS-er who received it. For inside the gay gold and red cover was a surprise valentine — a white, lacy heart, framing a snapshot of their beloved Juel, in her wheelchair. Nor was that all. In her arms she held a laughing baby, Helen's granddaughter, named Robin, after their magazine. Instantly, they all adopted the baby as their godchild!

The Round Robin has opened a new world to them all. Through its pages they learn the names and addresses of others in their town who have the disease. They visit with them on the telephone, and soon warm friendships are formed. They become like one big family, responding, family-style, to special needs.

When one goes into the hospital because of a setback, the news flies around, and all rally to cheer the patient. Mollie, the victim of a stroke, polio, and now MS, wrote from her hospital bed, "I want to thank all the many Robins who sent me cards, letters and oodles of get-well wishes. I had 76 cards! My nurse decorated both doors of the wardrobe with them. They meant much to me, for I knew each of them represented a cane, crutches, wheel chair or hospital bed."

The Round Robin inspires many a kindly act. "Don't forget big-hearted Jonesy," wrote a grateful MS-er to Editor Helen. "Gee! You've just got to meet him to appreciate all he does for others less fortunate than himself. He is able to walk with the help of a brace, but, best of all, he can drive a car. He takes three or four of us MS-ers out visiting other MS-ers.

I don't know what we would do without him. It just makes you feel so good to get out of the house."

Jonesy received the Robin award for such service to others — a feather to put in his cap!

Once a discouraged MS-er wrote, "All I can do is keep out of the way." Not any more! A friend sent her a *Round Robin*. Now she is happily one of the "flock," saving a penny a day to put in her Penny Pot, as her valiant bit to support MS research, and making tags from old Christmas cards, to sell for the same cause.

Not all their trips are to hospitals. One MS-er, for ten years a pilot, flies to his home field for a reunion with his old buddies. How the Robins love these travel letters! "Gives us all a sense of going places," writes a bedfast MS-er.

But they like, too, to hear about "the little things" that happen in one another's homes. They chuckle over the letter telling how the writer's four-year-old grandchild brought her a live mouse to keep her company. And at Emma's dilemma: "I'm still working on plans for my daughter's wedding. This week the minister of the church resigned and the orchestra called and said they have two engagements for the same date. Think I'll just put a ladder under the window and help her down. What do you think?"

The Round Robin gives them a place to share their headline news — a part-time job; or, at long last — Hurrah! Hurrah! — the winning of a contest. Also a place to share their small joys. "I received a lovely white poinsettia plant from a friend. When I was ready to throw it out, I noticed little leaves sprouting on it, and now I have something to watch grow."

The Round Robin gives them a place to air their troubles, sure of a sympathetic ear. Writes Zelma, "Another thing I do for no reason, as I have a very good husband, is cry. I know it's just nerves, but it's heck!"

Writes Agnes, in unusual complaint, "MS has affected my speech to such a degree that I only say absolutely essential things. My 10-year-old Dave has grown up with me in an almost silent world."

Worries Alice, "I've been having blackouts, resulting in many falls. I have become an occasional sleepwalker. I only hope I don't scare the kids." Explodes Dick, "My feet drag maddeningly."

The Round Robin gives them a place to tell their triumphs, too. Mildred had a sleeping sickness, and lay six months in bed, with doctors on the case saying she could not possibly live. When she finally stirred and opened her eyes, they found her body paralyzed by MS.

She exults, "Since 1942, I have learned to eat again, read, write, talk, and do most all things, except walk!"

Small triumphs are just as joyfully recorded. Writes Fanny, "I am doing real well for myself. A few weeks ago, I found I could stand for almost three minutes without holding on to anything."

Sometimes they try to tell what this cheery, chins-up little magazine means to them. Writes Jim,

"*The Round Robin* is a gold mine to me, in that I can unload the things that are bottled up in me, and feel that some MS-er will hear me through, even with interest, and not think me a bore."

Writes Rebecca, "*The Round Robin* brings us together in spirit." So closely that on occasions they unite in moments of silence, at a stated time, to help one of them who is faced with a crisis.

Writes Jane, "*The Round Robin* was a great big turning point in my life. The misery and loneliness, B.R. (Before Robin) seem unreal now."

All this, from a few letters — and Juel!

An Endless Chain

We stood on the church steps, visiting. My friend took out his wallet, opened it, and said, "Look!" There, among his other treasured snaps, was a billfold-sized, plastic-coated reproduction of Warner Sallman's first painting of the Head of Christ.

Looking at the little picture, I had a sudden feeling of being on holy ground; of feeling His Presence, His strength, virility, power and love.

"Oh," I said, "I wish I had one just like it!" Without a word, my friend took it out of his wallet and handed it to me.

"Oh, no!" I protested. "I didn't mean to ask for it."

"I'm glad you did," he assured me, gravely, "for that is the only way, under the plan, I could have given it to you. You see, you have to want it. We don't distribute these pictures like handbills. Now you are one of Carl Duning's endless chain of card-carrying Christians. There are hundreds of thousands of us!"

"But now you, yourself, don't have a picture of Christ, for your billfold," I protested.

"That's all part of the plan," he explained. "All I need do is write for another, and then, in turn, pass that one on to some interested person. You must do the same. Open your purse, someday soon, and show your little picture of Christ to a friend. Should he or she express a wish to have one, give it at once, and send for another. I keep a dozen on hand. It is such a simple sort of evangelism — and so sure!"

That is how I first learned about the Duning plan that has sparked the printing of more than a hundred million of these powerful little purse-sized pictures of Christ.

Later I was to meet the man responsible for the project which is now working its comradely way around the world.

"You may write about the 'Christ In Every Purse Plan,'" said Carl H. Duning, "but keep my name out of it. I'm not a preacher. I'm just a plain businessman!"

He was emphatic—this handsome, well-built man, with eyes as blue as summer skies, hair as white as the first soft snow, and the lilt of spring in his heart.

"But you were the originator of the plan, weren't you?"

"Give all the credit to God," he objected. "All I had was an idea."

"Which," I pointed out, "in less than three years, spread all over the United States, reached Canada, and leaped the seas to India, Japan, Norway, England and Germany."

Cornered, he admitted it. "But," he hedged, "let me emphasize that the 'Christ In Every Purse' plan is really the project of my church—St. John's Lutheran, Richmond, Indiana. It was the publicity of our own Luther Feeger and Ed Kaueper, newspaper men, that helped to spread it. And another of our men, Harry Tubesing, a printer, did the booklets. Our Sunday school gave $100 to help the project at the start. You can mention all of these. But keep my name out, will you?"

No, I thought. This is Carl H. Duning's story.

"Everything for the Home" is the slogan of the Duning Furniture Co., Inc., Richmond, Indiana. In the stock were large-size pictures of Warner Sallman's "Head of Christ."

"Where do you plan to hang this picture?" Duning would ask customers. If they said in some local church or Sunday school, he'd say, "Forget the price. I'll make you a present of it."

There was something about that particular picture of Christ that gripped Carl Duning. He had always imagined Christ looked like that—rugged, sun-tanned, lean and sinewy—every inch a man's man.

During World War II, when 76 young men from his church, all in active service, received their church letters, they found in each a small reproduction of Sallman's masterpiece. With the little picture was Carl's suggestion, "Keep this handy in your purse. It will help you in your thinking, reminding you always of His presence."

About three centuries ago, Brother Lawrence evolved a method for "practicing the presence of God" among the pots and pans of a monastery kitchen. The gift of the little picture of Christ was simply Carl's twentieth-century method for practicing that same saving Presence, even on the battle field.

Requests for more of the pictures came pouring in. From the fiery front, from blood-stained, weary veterans of Anzio, Consino, and Salerno. From a hospital, filled to capacity, after the Battle of the Bulge, where one wounded soldier shared his Bible and his little picture of Christ with his wardmates.

This soldier's mother came to see Carl—whose own three sons were in the service—to tell him of the saving grace of that one small picture, and how her son's close buddy had been converted and baptized, just a few days before he had been killed in action.

That set Carl thinking. If so small a thing worked so mightily for the Lord in war, why not also in peace? Why not launch a "Christ In Every Purse" campaign among civilians? No sooner thought than done. He outlined a plan as simple and sincere, as challenging and crusading as the picture itself. It reads:

1. Obtain a picture to carry in your purse.

2. Give the picture to an interested person, and obtain another.

3. Encourage your Sunday school or any other

organized church group to arrange for wider distribution.

4. Communicate with Carl H. Duning, Tenth and Main Streets, Richmond, Indiana, who will give you full information. There is no charge for information or use of the plan. Duning will inform you of the cost of the pictures.

"I was superintendent of our Sunday school when I started the 'Christ In Every Purse' campaign," recalled Carl Duning. "Little did I dream then how quickly it would spread beyond church, city, state and national boundary lines. Today, more than 50 foreign missionaries are using these prints. The appreciative letters I get from them for the help it gives them with the natives, is a wonderful reward!"

I asked him about the hundreds of speeches he has made about his "Christ In Every Purse" project.

"I am no speaker," he deplored. "I just talk." Just the same, he started giving local "chats" about the artist Sallman and his masterpiece, suggesting that his listeners carry in their purses or wallets this "reminder," and watch how it lifted their lives.

Sallman and he had become close friends. Both businessman and artist had grown up in Christian homes. In the heart of each burned a deep love for Christ. Duning found a spiritual outlet in church work, Sallman in Christian art.

While Sallman was a student at the Chicago Art Institute, an instructor advised him to attend classes in a Bible Institute, in order to obtain background for his work.

Unwittingly, the dean of this Bible Institute played a major part in giving all Christendom the rich ministry of Sallman's sacred artistry. For he told the aspiring young man to saturate his mind with the spirit of Christ, to study His life and message, and, with this as a background, to evolve a "Head of Christ" that would depict greater spiritual strength, virility and power than were shown in the conventional paintings of the Saviour.

The years sped by, and Sallman, now Art Editor for a religious publication for young people, was suddenly confronted with a difficult assignment. He was asked to draw a picture of the head of Christ — one that would "challenge and hold the interest of modern youth."

In vain, Sallman sought for the picture behind his closed lids. The days flew by, nearer and nearer to the dreaded deadline when he must deliver the drawing to the engraver. One can imagine how he wrestled in prayer.

Then, miraculously, the very night before the deadline, a clear and definite idea of a Christ head flashed into his mind. Quickly he put the lines on paper, and the next day made a drawing of his now famous "Head of Christ."

Inspired as it was, it inspired everyone who saw it. Encouraged by this, the young artist had one thousand copies of it made, to distribute as gifts.

He might have left it at that—he was a busy artist, with other commissions claiming his attention—had it not been for his friends. They wanted to see that beautiful Head of Christ done in oils. After sixteen years, he yielded to their requests.

Again, the response was immediate. The oil painting won wide acclaim in art circles, among clergymen and the general public, as a modern portrayal of the personality of Christ. Millions of copies of the painting, large and small, went out on their mission, a response, in their own lovely way, to the soul's quest, "We would see Jesus."

All this story behind the picture, Carl Duning wove into his "talks"—he will not let you call them "speeches"—and soon he found himself invited to speak before organizations as varied as Ministerial Associations, Alcoholics Anonymous, Luther League Conventions and Better Business Clubs.

Tens of thousands of the pictures were distributed as the local project became state-wide. The Kiwanians —Carl was then Lieutenant-Governor of the Indiana District—took it up through their Committee in Support of Churches. Young people's societies, church men's organizations, civic groups, all joined the endless chain for Christ.

The great ones of this and other lands sought out this "plain businessman" and his practical plan for remembering Christ. One was Dr. Tomiko Kora, member of the Upper House of the Japanese parliament, who was visiting this country after a tour of European capitals. She asked Carl Duning if he could take time to explain his campaign to her.

This cultured Christian Japanese, absorbed in such tremendously important projects as the raising of some

$10,000,000 in the United States and Canada toward the building of a great Christian university for Japan, listened attentively as Carl talked.

She asked for a supply of the pictures and booklets to take back with her to her country. Radiating the spirit of the Prince of Peace, they went quietly on their blessed mission.

I have on my desk a batch of requests Carl has received for purse-size pictures of Sallman's "Head of Christ." Many are from foreign countries. One is from Germany, from a pastor who asks in humble, broken English for 500 little pictures and 100 booklets.

Pinned to his first letter is a second, dated a year later. "Beloved brother in Christ," it reads, "Now I have a second asking—"

One smiles at the quaint phrase. Yet that is the secret of the amazing growth of this endless chain for Christ—just by another asking . . . and then another!

Here is one from Asia. The writer has found the story of the "Christ In Every Purse" project in a seven-year-old *Christian Herald*, and asks if it is too late now to get a picture. Carl sends her a dozen by return mail!

Here is a letter from a Methodist Mission in India, thanking Carl for his gift of pictures. "This work you are doing is somewhat different," he writes, "and very effective. May the Lord use these pictures to His glory and the blessing of many."

Some of the requests are from service chaplains, which seems very fitting, for the project started as a tribute to the young men of Carl's church who were in military service during World War II; and Carl's booklet, "Christ In Every Purse," is dedicated to these men, among them the four who gave their lives for their country, one of whom was Carl's own son and namesake.

In the Duning office are files that bulge with letters from humble Christians who are seeking a closer walk with God. Also impressive scrapbooks of celebrities' letters, all commending his plan, many from distinguished authors and speakers, teachers and preachers. But letters come, too, from the Lord's less articulate ones, who find the little pictures speak for them. As, for instance, this from Beryl of Hastings, Nebraska, "I am quite a reticent person—a reserved Presbyterian. Not at all able to evangelize. But I feel in this way I can spread the gospel of Christ in an effective way. I am grateful to you for the idea, which has brought me much joy in putting it to work."

Yes, each picture is a silent evangelist. "I work with a tough gang," a mechanic told me, as he fixed my garage plumbing, "but just the thought of that picture in the pocket of my jeans helps steer me straight."

"It made me a tither," confided a big executive.

"It helps to keep me a Christian all week," a lively Luther Leaguer soberly explained.

Carl Duning spoke in my church a few months ago. His doctor has told him to slow down, so that he has retired, and left the operation of his business to his sons.

"That's fine!" he said. "Now I can give all my time to the Christ In Every Purse campaign."

"It's a wonderful plan—" I began.

"Give all the credit to God," he reminded me again. "All I had was an idea."

Floyd Starr—You Must Meet Him!

The telephone broke the silence of my Miami home. Over the line rushed the lyric voice of our church soprano, eager, excited: "Floyd Starr! You **must** meet him! He's my friend's guest . . . here for just a short stay . . . President of the Starr Commonwealth for Boys, near Albion, Michigan. May I bring him over?"

I said "Do!" as one in a dream, my thoughts leaping the years to a far-distant day when I'd stood on the deck of a ship that was bringing me to America for the first time, listening to a fellow passenger saying those words to me, about the selfsame man! "Floyd Starr! You must meet him."

I closed my eyes and, in imagination, heard again the kindly voice of that New York minister at my elbow—sorry for any poor tourist bound for Detroit. "But since you're doomed to six weeks of it," he had smiled, "here are four newsworthy men you should meet while there."

He jotted the names down on the back of his card.

59

"The last," he mused, "is a foolish young fellow named Starr, who insists that there is no such thing as a bad boy!"

He turned from the vastness of the sea—wide as God's mercy—to repeat thoughtfully, "Floyd Starr. You must meet him. Because that foolish young man might be right!"

In Detroit, I'd easily interviewed all but young Starr. I never could catch up with him. Finally I'd stopped trying. But I had never forgotten him. Even when my summer trip had lengthened into a permanent stay in America, Starr had stuck in the back of my mind, as a bit of unfinished business.

And now, by mere chance—or was it by the Lord's plan?—I was to get that interview for which I'd waited so many years!

The door chimes rang—and suddenly I was shaking hands with Dr. Floyd Starr, a tall, well-built, handsome man, with a distinguished bearing and gracious manner. He looked at me long and searchingly, then smiled.

Those eyes! They are a magnetic grey, with stars in them that glow, brood, sparkle or twinkle, according to his mood. A wealth of grey hair rose like a crest from a high, fine forehead—hair so electric with life that I half expected it to shoot sparks when he smoothed it back with strong, swift hands—the same hands that had ploughed and dug, baked and scrubbed when the Commonwealth was young and the going hard.

I told of the occasion when I had first heard of him. Instantly he was off in a rush of happy memories, his voice unforgettable in its deep, rich resonance.

"That was the year I launched Starr Commonwealth. I started with two homeless boys who hitchhiked to find me. We all slept on the hay in the barn of the forty-acre farm I had just bought with my own money."

He stopped to picture the weather-beaten little barn for me. "It leaked—that only roof we had! The rain dripped down on us. We could look up and see a star shining through a wide crack. The farm had no homestead, no plumbing, no electricity—just plenty of weeds and cobblestones. But it had a little lake over which the sun set in a glory of color, some rolling hills, the two-story barn—and my two waifs. That was the beginning."

Such a tiny acorn from which to grow so mighty an oak! Two boys, then—and now, as I write, there are two hundred living in the Commonwealth, and in its two branches, one of which is in Ohio. And in the half century during which the school has operated, no less than five thousand destitute, disgraced or delinquent boys have gone out from this, their "other home," to demonstrate the good that Starr insisted was in them. Over ninety per cent have proved he was right! Some as ministers, college professors, high school principals, lawyers, athletes, newspaper men, choir directors, musicians, licensed state surveyors, besides countless well-trained farmers and industrial workers. One old Starr boy is a newsreel cameraman with Para-

mount; another is one of the nation's leading criminol-
ogists; and still another is the very successful director
of the Ohio branch of the Commonwealth.

"When did you move out of the barn?" I asked.

"As soon as I built our first cottage—on the ruins
of the former burnt-out farmhouse. That was in 1913.
It was a simple white frame structure, but my heart
was in every plank and stone of it. I named it Gladsome Cottage, because it was such a gladsome thing to
have really started, at last, to make my dream come
true."

At last! Why, at that time, he could have been little
more than a lad himself—that foolish young man with
a strange conviction!

"Dr. Starr," I interrupted, "When did you first have
this idea of yours to save boys?"

"When I was four." His eyes were twinkling, but
he meant it. He was that age when he heard his parents discussing how Dr. John Harvey Kellogg had
adopted fifty children. Next day he capped a score of
questions with one more, "Mother, what means
adopted?"

And she — God bless all patient mothers who answer the questions of little boys! — had explained it
so persuasively that from then on Floyd knew what
he was going to do when he grew up. He was going to
adopt fifty friendless children!

His childhood ambition stayed with him through
high school and college. He knew by then the type of
child he most wanted to help—boys who were in trou-

ble because they were deserted, destitute, or the delinquent result of broken homes or the wrong sort of parents. He chose studies that would help him understand the problem boy.

One day, with graduation near, a fraternity brother asked, "What are your plans, Starr? We never hear you say."

"I'm going to buy a small farm, and adopt a lot of homeless children—the sort nobody wants."

What a laugh went up! But young Starr was in dead earnest. Here, before the glowing log fire, relaxing with his good college friends, he told for the first time, his cherished dream.

But that was the day when the "first offender" was considered a young criminal, sentenced to long years in a reform school; garbed in institutional uniform; put on silence all day; locked up all night; repressed by a score of rigid rules, for the breaking of which were harsh punishments, including floggings and the deadlier dungeon.

No wonder his college pals were skeptical! Take kids from the streets, the juvenile courts, broken homes and unspeakable environments, and raise them in normal homes, with no bars or bolts! *Bad boys!*

"There is no such thing as a bad boy!" flamed young Floyd Starr, never dreaming that he had formulated the first article of his now-famous creed, which starts with those very words, adding: "We believe that badness is not a normal condition but the fruit of misdirected energy."

He wrote the creed before a stone of the present great Commonwealth was in place. To date, it has reformed, from the inside out, thousands of so-called "bad boys," among them thieves, forgers, bandits, gang leaders, and young toughs who were the terror of home, school, community and the police. Somehow Starr has loved them all into shape!

"They weren't bad boys," he explained to me. "Each had some kink in his character that needed to be straightened out. It took time, of course, and a lot of patience, and sometimes heartache, to find out why he was wayward. But, sooner or later, we were working at that kink together. For every normal boy deep down in his heart wants to be good."

As I listened enthralled to this radiant man, who one minute has the buoyancy of a boy and the next, the dignity of a bishop, I rejoiced with him at the way God had blessed his venture.

At first, forty stony acres, yielding only two sparse crops to feed healthy young appetites. "Oh," groaned Starr, "those everlasting beans and boiled potatoes!"

Now a 50-acre campus and a 2500-acre farm, growing scores of varieties of farm and garden produce! A fine herd of full-blooded, registered Holsteins, a modern dairy, thousands of Leghorn chickens! All the fresh vegetables, pasteurized milk, farm butter, and fresh eggs, that one hundred and sixty boys—many of whom arrive undernourished—can eat!

At first, one simple white frame cottage, called "Gladsome." Now fifteen, each a home in the truest sense of the word. Five are Old English-type, vine-covered dwellings that might well be those of an exclusive private school. Two are ranch-type cottages. Then there are seven off-campus remodeled farm houses, which the boys love because they are small homes where eight to twelve lads make up the "family." Some even have barns where the boys can keep their pets.

Building upon building—all gifts from a true democracy of donors. From a fund; a foundation; from a Palm Beach bank president; from a local handy-man who loved boys and left his life savings to buy a little farmhouse to shelter eight homeless incorrigibles. From a society matron; a working housemother; an osteopathic physician; a wealthy man of the world; a young architect who, after spending one challenging day at the Commonwealth, hurried home to persuade his good mother to donate a badly needed new cottage.

And, in more recent years, from a distinguished judge, in gratitude for all Starr had done for lads brought to his court; from a grieving mother who gave the cottage as a memorial to her teen-age son; and from the late Ruth Bryan Rohde—the boys' beloved "Aunt Ruth"—a member of the 71st and 72nd Congresses, Minister Plenoptentiary to Denmark, and an alternate representative of the 4th General Assembly of the UN.

The very beauty of the campus is a gift; for, in 1917, T. Glenn Phillips, noted landscape architect of Detroit, drew plans for the entire grounds and buildings as his "missionary gift for the year."

I smiled at Floyd Starr, reminiscing so happily on my porch. I was glad that I had met him! I remembered how away back in 1913, a judge had called him "a crackpot with a knuckle-headed idea."

I remembered, too, how at a recent Testimonial Dinner, Judge George Edwards of the Michigan State Supreme Court of Justice had said:

"We are here to testify to the character which Starr Commonwealth has built into the lives of thousands of boys; and to the man who has opened to them their Door to Hope.... There was the boy who one day came to Floyd Starr, with hands thrust arrogantly in his pockets, a sneer twisting his lips, to snarl, 'You can't do nothin' with me, mister!' That boy is now a minister. There was the lad who boasted that he was the smartest car thief in Michigan. That youth is now a teacher of college sociology. There was the kid who slept on the alley grating because he had no other place to go. He now heads up a successful business of his own. Starr has given them all a pattern for living."

But as Starr sat on my porch that day, his thoughts were still on the early days of struggle. He spoke ruefully of their first schoolhouse—the tar-paper shanty where they froze in winter, and sweltered in summer. And before that, a cluttered corner of Gladsome, where Starr — all the teaching staff there was — had to dismiss school when the table — all the desk there was — was needed for the frugal meal of homemade bread, lard, beans and potatoes.

Now, by a miraculous answer to prayer, there is a fine modern school building, overlooking the lake; well-equipped and staffed, taking the boys through the eleventh grade; and for the advanced boys, both in character and scholarship, spacious Reynolds Hall, in Jackson, Michigan, where they can finish high school and complete the first two years of college.

They bring honor to Starr, these off-the-campus students. Of the six graduating from Jackson High, one year, Peter was on the *cum laude* list; Reeves was graduated *magna cum laude*, and Henry was the president of the senior class of 398, and was offered scholarships by seven colleges!

"Dreams do come true—when you work as well as dream," Starr smiled. "Right now, we are praying for a little chapel."

I followed him through the years, keeping in touch. Always he had another goal ahead; something else to dream into reality, for his boys. A shop, in which to learn a trade, to start them on their way to make an honest living. A physical education building for the bigger boys who were now coming to the school, who needed man-size equipment. A chapel!

The "Little Chapel-in-the-Woods"! Oh, the years they longed and prayed for it! Starr and his boys had worshipped in so many strange places. In the barn days, beside the lake—the sunset, their stained-glass windows; the stars, their altar candles.

In Gladsome Cottage, they had prayed together, in summer, under the trees; in winter, beside the kitchen fire. Then, as the family kept growing in numbers, they had worshipped in the basement; and later, in their first little tar-paper school. Finally, in Webster Hall, a fine building, but one that had to serve many other purposes.

"I want my boys," Starr said, his eyes full of a great longing, "to have holy memories of a little sanctuary on the campus; of stained glass windows, a white altar. Sometimes it takes just such a memory to keep a tempted boy on the straight path."

They had to wait for years for this dream to be realized, but at long last, on a beautifully-wooded piece of donated land, their Little Chapel in the Woods was built. It was dedicated October 3, 1950 — thirty-seven years to the day after Starr had come to his little rundown farm. Like the rest of the Commonwealth, it is a treasury of gifts. Every jeweled window is a memorial. The Connsonata organ is a gift. The lovely little chapel, itself, is the gift of donors, rich and poor. A prisoner serving time in jail, earning twenty cents a day, spent it all to buy wood he fashioned into jewel boxes, to be sold for the chapel fund.

The old boys came back in droves for Home Day, the Sunday of the impressive chapel dedication week. They had been invited to bring their babies to be baptized in the new little chapel, where their "Uncle Floyd" could hold the silver bowl, and so add loving meaning to the important event.

Among the old boys who crossed the nation to attend the dedication was a prosperous businessman who went from one new building to another, saying, "I remember when—" He was one of the two little waifs who slept in the barn.

Said a reporter to me, "You know, I envy this guy, Starr. He has found something big enough to live and die for."

The little barn still stands, not far from the fine buildings of the Commonwealth—like the humble little mother of a thriving, stalwart family. Standing before it, you remember the sweet-smelling hay those first little waifs slept on, with their new-found friend and savior. You think of the star they saw through the broken roof.

And, suddenly, you remember the manger-hay of a stable of old, and a Star above it that foretold salvation.

It is as if the little barn wanted to remind you of another friend of sinners, who went about doing good, and held in His loving heart, a purpose big enough to live and die for.

This creed written in 1913 just before the SCB was founded is still in the vanguard of performance among similar projects for teen-aged offenders.

STARR COMMONWEALTH CREED

Written by Floyd Starr in 1913

WE BELIEVE that there is no such thing as a bad boy.

WE BELIEVE that badness is not a normal condition but is the result of misdirected energy.

WE BELIEVE that every normal boy will be good if given an opportunity in an environment of love and activity.

WE BELIEVE in the dignity of labor. We believe that each child should be given some work suitable to childhood and that he should be taught that the value of labor is to be found, not alone in the completed task, but in the training of the mind and the hand, and in the joy of accomplishment.

WE BELIEVE also in play. Play is the child's normal means of self-expression.

WE BELIEVE that to attain the full stature of man, spiritual development should go hand in hand with physical, mental, and moral development.

WE BELIEVE that boys should be treated, not as a class, but as individuals, and that each boy in order that he may reach his highest development, must be understood. We hold that his ambition must be stimulated and developed, and that he must be encouraged and loved toward perfection.

WE BELIEVE that boys merit confidence and trust, and that the secret of the development of honor in a boy lies in appealing to his inherent goodness. In order that he may attain perfect manhood, we believe in placing a boy on his honor at all times and giving him the sympathy and encouragement necessary to enable him to maintain his integrity.

My Star in the East

She did not look like a star—this small, brown sparrow of a Welsh woman. There was nothing brilliant about her, none of the qualities that makes for a following. She was just part of the usual background of Sunday, as it was lived in the English village where I grew up.

Yet, looking back, with half a century and the Atlantic Ocean between, I know that Elizabeth Rees was my Star in the East—the one, above all others, who, unknowingly, led me along the straight, sure path to Jesus.

In those days, in that hard-working village, one day in seven was religiously given to Heaven. By eight-thirty in the morning, we children were in Sunday school. By ten-thirty, we were trudging in a long "crocodile" of twos to the ancient parish church, for morning service. Miss Rees, in her plain tweed suit and square-toed shoes, strode alongside, timing our pace to the distant church bells.

The seniors led the line, which dwindled down in

size and strength to the tail, where the tots did their valiant best to keep up.

Once when I was about five years old, and the last in line, Miss Rees gathered my weary, weaving feet into her arms, and carried me the last quarter mile. That is the first time I remember her. That is how all the villagers remembered her. Not until they needed a lift did they know she was there.

By two o'clock we were in Sunday school again, and by seven-thirty, in church for the evening service. Miss Rees, in the queer hat which was the laughing stock of the Manor ladies, would perform all her routine duties as unobtrusively as possible. She had a positive genius for merging into the background. She would sound the tuning fork for the Sunday school's chanting of the creed, check the pulpit candles, admonish the drowsy boy who "blew" the organ. It was a pity, I would hear the vestry men whisper, that the vicar's sister was such a plain person—but she was a great help to him, of course.

In the slow course of childhood years, I reached Miss Rees' class. Each Sunday morning I dutifully repeated to her, from memory, the collect and the Gospel for the day; each Sunday afternoon, the Epistle and some great religious poem, chosen by her. "Ode to Duty" or "Crossing the Bar" were her favorites.

I liked her quiet "Well done," but she was still outside my life, as impersonal a part of Sunday as the chimes and the collect.

Once I was gratefully conscious of her, in a speechless sort of way. I was in a scrape. I did not understand what I was charged with, but I knew by my father's stern face, as he stood shoulder to shoulder with the judges, that it was something unspeakably bad.

Every year the squire of the village, who had once written a book, offered prizes for the best original essay and the best original poem entered by a resident of the village. Children were not supposed to compete, but I submitted a poem, the brainchild of much anguished mental travail.

On the great evening when the efforts were read in the village schoolhouse and the awards made, the judges questioned my right to the half-guinea reward. They said no child of my age could possibly have written that poem; that I must have copied it from a book or magazine.

Faced by the dreadful new word "plagiarism," with no dictionary near me, I was going down for the third time in a sea of confusion that looked suspiciously like guilt, when Elizabeth threw me a rope in the quiet question, "On what did you make your first copy of this poem?"

"On a sugar bag."

"If I took you home, could you find it, and bring it here?"

"Of course."

In twenty minutes we were back, my hands clutching grocery sacks on which I had scribbled my many attempts to write the prize poem. It was positive evidence of my authorship. My father relaxed, my mother smiled, the judges applauded. Miss Rees? I don't remember! She must have merged into the background when she was no longer needed.

Elizabeth Rees did not come into my life until my world went out, with the sudden death of my mother. This was the first great grief of my life, casting me on a sea of such bleak heartbreak as only an unsure, sensitive child of thirteen can know.

There had been only four in our family—my parents, my sister and I. My mother, young, gay and radiant, had been our sunshine. Without her, my stricken dad retreated yet deeper into the recesses of his silent self; my sister, older than I, into complete absorption in her studies. I alone seemed to have no defense against this terrible new aching emptiness, this abysmal loneliness. I had not yet learned to seek solace in writing. All seemed lost.

My family tried to help—my dad, with competent housekeepers, my sister by urging me to a "decent show of fortitude." But I seemed to have turned to stone inside. I could not cry. A numb hopelessness settled down on me like a fog, as the black-garbed weeks crept by.

The home I had loved so much seemed now an empty shell. When the time came to go to the seaside, I spent hours on the white cliffs, watching the waves beat against a jagged, scarred rock. That rock, I thought, is my heart, the waves, my grief.

One grey, stormy day, I turned to discover I was no longer alone. Elizabeth Rees was sitting on a nearby boulder, gazing out to sea. She had come clear across England to seek me out!

She never said a word, just sat there, her eyes closed against the high wind, her strong, square hands cupped over her tweeded knees, her square-toed oxfords, scuffed with tramping, firmly planted together.

Slowly I went to her. She made room for me on her boulder. I smelled the tweediness of her coat, and remembered the time when she had carried me over the last quarter mile. The ice within me began to thaw.

Suddenly the storm, long brewing, swept the sea at which we gazed. The waves swelled and rolled and crashed. And there, right in the swell of a huge breaker, was a fisherman's little boat! I cried out for the frail thing's safety.

Miss Rees' voice came to me, calm as a dove, through the spray of the gale. "Don't worry. She'll come safely to harbor . . ."

Long after the little boat had ridden out the storm, Miss Rees sat there, quietly talking to me about life, and courage to weather its storms.

"If the sails of one's soul are set right," she told me in her serene, sure voice, "one will come safely to heaven, never fear."

Ah! That was what I wanted! For my mother was in heaven.

Fearfully I asked, "How do I set them right—the sails of my soul?"

"What were your mother's last words to you?" asked Miss Rees, her eyes far off to sea. "Don't tell me if you'd rather not."

But, surprisingly, I wanted to. Just talking to some-one like this, who was so kind, and yet kept her distance, brought to me a strange comfort, a warmth. Tears flooded my eyes. The relief of them, the release!

"She whispered, 'Good-by, Kitten. Be good . . . always.' She always called me 'Kitten' when she was especially loving me."

Miss Rees took from the pocket of her tweed coat a worn, slim green book. "I use it daily," she said. "Prayer is the surest way I know of setting the sails of one's soul right. That is what helps me most."

Prayer was the secret, she told me, of victory, of the power to see things through, of heartsease. Not just the prayers one prayed in church, but everyday prayers as one went about one's work and play.

This was a new Miss Rees. Her words poured out, eager and eloquent. Her calm brown eyes had golden sparks in them, like stardust. Then—I never knew how it happened—we were down on our knees together, by the boulder, as if before a church altar, and I was praying away, in halting words, all the bitter rebellion, the stony loneliness of my little-girl heart.

Kneeling there, I glimpsed, for the first time, the glory of a religion like Elizabeth's, which one lived daily—quietly, simply, completely, giving all one was, and all one had.

Although I did not know it then, she had shown me the Way, just as miraculously as had the Star of Old, and had set my young feet upon it.

I was twenty-five when I sailed for America.

Among my flowers and gay bon voyage gifts was a small, drab package wrapped in a paper sack, tied with grocery string.

I opened it with curious fingers. Inside was a slim book of prayers, similar to the one Elizabeth Rees had taken from her pocket that long-ago day on the cliffs. She had carefully bound it in sailcloth, as a reminder of the little boat we had watched ride out the storm, and come safely to harbor. On the fly-leaf she had written the one word, "Kitten."

It is on my desk as I write this. Its leaves are frayed from daily use. Its cover has been twice replaced. It has traveled back and forth across the ocean with me. It has been hidden under my pillow in sick room and hospital. It is my treasured spiritual compass, the greatest guiding power in my life, next to my Bible.

Because of all it symbolizes, I have taught classes of teen-agers, in churches of half a dozen different denominations, praying that I may pass on something of what Elizabeth Rees gave me.

I Belong to the King

The Story of a Backwoods Hymn-writer,
and Miss Kohler's Young People

Ida L. Reed, hymn-writer of another generation, came into my life when she was old and feeble, her health broken by severe illnesses and the desperate struggle of years to wrest a living from a small, stony farm in the hills of West Virginia.

I had written an article called, "Hymns We Love To Sing" for *Christian Herald*. In the mail following its appearance was a letter from this old writer of Gospel songs and hymns. It had about it a spiritual aura. I kept it in my Bible for days. It seemed to belong there.

Did I know, the letter asked, "I Belong to the King"? Because that was one of her best-known hymns. In its day, four million copies of it had been sold. It had appeared in thirty different hymn collections. Thousands of books containing it had been sold in England, and it had been translated into Scandinavian and German.

The letter went on to tell of her present life, revealing more than she ever knew. All the lack and loneliness it held were there between the lines.

"I shall never, in all probability, have enough to take away the dread of my tomorrows," she confided, "or the shadow of my last days, but I am deeply grateful that God called me to do my humble best for the Kingdom."

That Sunday, I heard "I Belong to the King" soaring through the stained-glass windows of a magnificent church in my home city. And I thought of the destitute writer of it, alone and forgotten, yet going bravely on, asking nothing of a world that so soon forgets.

A few evenings later, another of her hymns, "Somebody's Praying For You," came over the radio. That night I could not sleep. Untold thousands of souls had been saved or strengthened by this hymn, yet who was praying for her? Who was giving her a helping hand over the last sad stretch of the road where all the milestones are gravestones?

I decided to write to her regularly; to slip in a five-dollar bill when I could, bitterly conscious that it was not enough.

Thus began a correspondence, stretching over the years. I would cry over her letters, then dry my eyes quickly, lest my tears should seem like pity, and affront the proud sensitiveness of a poor little lady of the Old South. She had sent me a picture of her tiny frame house. Back of it rose the hills, and before it a steep road. Nothing else. I tried to persuade myself that the faded print showed a cabin in the distance from which smoke might rise up for company on the long, lonely nights of a mountain winter.

I learned about her afflicted, careworn past from her letters, and a simple little self-published book she sent me—her "Life." I have it before me now, each labored page dotted with her inked-in corrections.

As a child she had shared the heavy toil, and the hardships and privations that were the common lot of those who lived in isolated hill settlements in those early days. The help of all hands was needed by their ailing father, who later died of the dreaded "White Plague." For the thin little farm had to yield enough to furnish food for all of them, with a sufficient surplus to trade for other household necessities, and to pay enough on the mortgage to insure a roof over their heads.

But the child Ida had a secret "Star of Hope." It was her dream to one day escape "the prison of the hills" and to go away to school. The dream was fostered by her chance to read, in snatched minutes of leisure, the papers and magazines dropped off weekly at her home, to be called for later by those who lived at a great distance.

When she was about fifteen, her dream crystallized into a practical plan. She knew she would have to earn the money to go away to school. Why not study hard at home so that when she was old enough she could take the examination that would qualify her to teach in their little district school? The short winter term lasted only four months. By teaching, she could earn enough to attend the summer term in some nearby Normal School. She must study . . . study . . . study!

But soon she was too blind to study, for an epidemic of diphtheria in a most savage form, swept the hills, leaving in its wake the dead and the "half-dead" — children crippled with temporary paralysis and partial blindness. It left Ida with her young hair threaded with grey, and doomed to suffer the rest of her life from the weakening after-effects of the disease.

But the black cloud had a silver lining, for now she was too weak to shoulder her usual share of heavy farm tasks, and when her eyes grew strong enough, she had time to read and study. "Dear God," she prayed, "help me to pass that examination, get a first-grade certificate, and teach at home."

For two years she taught. Now she had earned enough to pay her way for a spring and summer term at the Normal School!

But her brother came to her while she was busy with her plans. "Ida," he pleaded, "could you lend Father your school money? He needs it badly. Our funds are running low."

Who knew better than she the back-breaking struggle he was making to survive? With hope deferred, she settled down to more months of grinding study, necessary if she was to meet the competition of other aspirants who had superior educational advantages—all eager to grasp this, their only chance to earn money in the backwoods.

She again passed her examination, and this time signed a contract to teach in a district school away from home. But a few weeks before it opened, she was stricken with another devastating illness, which her physician called brain fever.

Again it was a fight for her life, mercifully short, and again she was pulled through, although from that day she never knew what it was to be entirely free of pain and weakness. Yet, depleted as she was, she taught the whole winter term, helped through her worst days by some of her pupils who were as old as she was.

At the end of that hard winter, there was not enough money left for Normal School. Her "Star of Hope" no longer shone so brightly, but it still glimmered. There was a small select school in nearby Philippi. She could afford a few weeks of tuition there. It meant a mile to walk in all weathers, a dangerously swollen mountain river to cross, another long walk from the station to the school, a late hour to arrive for the first class, and a too-early hour to leave. But what did that matter? She was away at school!

She had barely settled into her little rented room when she became so desperately ill that two doctors had to be hastily called to her bedside. Added to her heartbreak was the galling knowledge that the family resented having a sick stranger in their home.

Never was she to forget that hopeless hour. Eight miles from her home, with a raging river between, with no way of sending a message to her parents, she somehow managed to dress, to pack up her few possessions, and creep along, a few halting steps at a time, to the school building to collect her books for the agonizing trip home.

Twenty years old, and she did not care whether she lived or died. No more dreaming. She must face reality. Two doctors and her teacher had convinced her of the utter hopelessness of ever again trying to go away to school. There could be no Normal College in the future—no longer any "Star of Hope."

As she neared the waiting room of the little station, she heard the gay laughter of carefree students gathered there. She could not face them. The train was in the station; the coach open. She could be alone there.

Not alone. For all the long struggle of the past, with its broken dreams, thwarted plans and dead hopes went with her, as well as the doubt, the dread, the hopelessness of the future.

"And there," she wrote, "in that bitter hour, I went down on my face before God, crushed and helpless. I gave up at last all my own will, my own plans, leaning entirely on His strength, willing to do and bear anything He willed, if only He would stand by and help me, and strengthen my soul to endure until He would set me free."

And, as she sobbed there, she felt the Presence . . . heard the still, small voice . . . and the Call!

"Oh, how He came to me," she wrote, "in all the fullness of His love and peace! There, in that hour, He promised me, surely and definitely, a greater blessing than that which I had lost—a fuller life of more blessed service than I had planned for myself. And more, He called me to the work that I have since done for Him. I can as easily doubt the fact that I exist as to doubt the truth of these things."

A few weeks after her return home, a young brother suggested, "Ida, why don't you write something for *The West Virginia Protestant*?" It was a publication he enjoyed reading. To please him, she wrote a poem, and mailed it. To her surprise, it was accepted—and so she saw the first of future thousands of her religious verses in print. Encouraged, she submitted another poem. This was not only accepted, but later set to music.

A few months after, she received a letter from the editor of the Sunday school periodicals of the Methodist Protestant Church, published at Pittsburg, Pa., who said he had read with pleasure her contribution to the *Protestant*, and wondered if he might not enlist her talent as an occasional contributor to their publications. He told her of the wide field of usefulness she might have in doing so, since the papers had a circulation of 30,000 to 35,000.

The "Star of Hope" glowed again! This great editor from the big world beyond the hills thought she had talent! Joyfully, she sent him some of her work, which he praised highly, and paid for in writing paper, stamps and a generous bundle of Sunday school papers and lesson leaves.

Much as she needed real money, she welcomed his "pay," for she was again teaching in the district school, and with the bright, cheery little papers, with their helpful stories, interesting articles and beautiful illustrations, she had the necessary material to start a Sunday school.

She held it every Friday afternoon in the day school with all the children, from tots to teens, crowded into its one room, and she, herself, all the staff there was. As a crowning joy, each child was given one of the pretty leaflets to take home and keep as his "very own."

Twenty years later she was to meet church and community leaders who told her that they still kept among their treasures those precious Sunday school papers of their youth.

And, although she did not realize it then, that little Sunday school for which she wrote both prose and poetry for its special occasions, was preparing her for the hundreds of Sunday school programs which she was later to write for the country's leading publishers of such material.

In the summer of 1887, she was finally able to attain her heart's desire. She attended the National Normal University at Lebanon, Ohio. True, it was only for three months, but to the eager Ida, it was the inspiration of a lifetime, for here she met dedicated young Christians from all over the country, many of whom were preparing for the mission field.

And that summer was also a revelation to her, for she discovered that, because of her life-long love of reading and her retentive memory, she was little behind in scholarship of all these bright young people. The knowledge gave her a confidence she had always lacked.

Back home in the hills, she taught one more year, and with her earnings bought something she yearned for, and needed for her hymn-writing—a little organ!

That year, she sent her first hymns to a music publisher, Fillmore Brothers of Cincinnati. She braced herself to face their rejection. Instead, they were accepted, and paid for, and the publishers recommended her work to others. As a result, she received a letter from the then well-known composer, Frank M. Davis, asking her for contributions to a book of sacred music he was compiling.

Soon she was writing by request several hymns for the evangelist, D. B. Towner, followed by requests from several publishers of books of hymns and sacred songs, and in the busy years that followed, she composed music or words—or both—for such well known publishers as The Hall-Mack Company of Philadelphia, Pa.; Dr. H. L. Gilmour, of Wenonah, N. J.; George F. Rosche Co., of Chicago, Ill.; Professor William J. Kirkpatrick, of Philadelphia, Pa.; and the Lorenz Company, Dayton, Ohio.

It was good that she could earn a little with her music—which she sold outright, without retaining copyrights—for her father, ill for many years of tuberculosis, was rapidly failing. Wrote Ida Reed, "His death was shadowed by one great grief—the insecurity of the debt-encumbered home, and the dread of homelessness for his loved ones, should it be sold by creditors."

When he died, that terrible fear was passed on to Ida, now forced to take his place as manager of the farm. In the home lived her mother and two sisters, none of whom had any income. The sons had long since left to earn a living elsewhere.

There followed years of heroic struggle as she strove to hold things together with her small irregular earnings of a dollar here, two dollars there; never enough. Yet some of her best hymns—she called them "heart cries"—were written during these burdened days. They came to her at odd times—as she was leading a sick horse home to be cared for; in the dark corner of a deserted church; in a railway station; as she worked in field or orchard; from the pages of a magazine.

It was the last-named that inspired her best known hymn, "I Belong to the King." Some kind friend had sent her a gift subscription to the *Christian Herald*. One day, after hard farm labor, she came to her organ for rest, and there beside it was a copy of the magazine, containing a serial called "A Princess In Calico," one she especially loved because the "Princess" was a hill-country girl, as she was, faced with the same hardships, frustrations and limitations.

In the story, a friend of this backwoods heroine had introduced her to a lovable invalid who had asked, "Does she belong to the King?" Meaning "Is she a Christian?"

As the work-worn farm woman at the little organ listlessly leafed through the pages of the magazine, those words seemed to leap out at her. Her fingers moved gently over the keys, as line by line, stanza by stanza, came to her, and so was born the hymn, "I Belong to the King," widely used in the Epworth League and other young people's church groups.

Ida Reed's little mother died in 1906, her end hastened by the death from tuberculosis of her youngest son, a minister of the United Brethren Church who, like Ida, had refused to give up, and had occupied his pulpit to within a week of his death.

Now there was no need to struggle to save the old farm. Her mother no longer needed its shelter. She had come at last to the inevitable breaking up of the only home she had ever known.

She spent the last summer in the fields, the orchards and the hills. "There is hardly a thicket or out-of-the-way corner of the fields," she was to write later, "scarcely a cluster of trees or a covert of woods, hardly a corner of the old barn that was not dear to me, because God met me there, and gave me an answer to my prayer, when I cried to Him in anguish of soul for help, new strength and grace to endure the almost intolerable burden."

On leaving the lost farm, Miss Reed rented a little frame cottage on the extreme outskirts of Philippi, where she hoped she could do much writing. At last, she had leisure; she was near lifelong friends all interested in her creativeness; she could attend church; perhaps collect her hymns into a book; she could live what was left of her own life!

Two weeks in the little haven, and then she was stricken with another of those terrible illnesses that had plagued her since her youth. Alone, but for the fleeting visits of her busy friends, she grew rapidly worse. Afraid of drifting into unconsciousness, she set her mind to thinking of a theme for a new hymn, and through the mists of pain and weakness came the refrain of "Somebody's Praying For You."

Line by line she repeated the verses over and over the long night through, afraid they might slip her fevered memory. Later she scribbled them in pencil, as best she could, and sent them to the Hall-Mack Company by whom they were copyrighted in 1907. The hymn's melody was written by C. Austin Miles, who wrote words and music for the ever-popular "In The Garden."

Ida Reed called "Somebody's Praying For You" her "song in the night." There were many more such songs, for the nights came thick and fast for the frail little hymn-writer. Five months of illness were spent in the home of a friend, only to learn that she must seek surgical aid at once.

Then to the Sibley Memorial Hospital in Washington, D. C., to undergo a serious operation, followed by five months of slow convalescence; then to be gently told that they could do no more for her, and it would be better for her to go home.

Home? To die? To that little rented cottage on the lonely hill? When she could not even walk yet, barely stand alone? How could she take care of herself? How earn a living? How pay the rent? She who had borne the burdens of her family found the thought intolerable that she must now be a burden to others.

When she arrived at the home station she was almost dead from collapse. A waiting friend took the limp, cold hymn-writer to her own comfortable home, and there put her to bed, still in her winter wrap, and buried her under a heap of blankets and in the midst of hot irons.

Four months she stayed in the home of that compassionate friend, under whose skillful care she found strength to stand, even to walk a few steps, only again to be forced to enter a hospital. Then a spine specialist gave her treatments that enabled her to walk without reeling and so perform the necessary small tasks in her little rented home.

But not for long. In October, 1911, she entered the German Hospital in Philadelphia, Pa., for still another operation. Seven weeks there, and then four months of slow recovery in a minister's home; and then back home again, weak, white and weary, to her little rented cottage.

Throughout these years of suffering she never ceased to write her hymns. While she was in Sibley Memorial Hospial, a few days before she was to undergo her operation—with slight hope that she could survive it—she wrote, "Leave me not alone."

While recovering in her friend's home, she wrote, "Sunshine Always," tracing the words in the blank leaves of her little Bible which lay where she could reach it from her bed.

But back in the little rented home she found writing difficult. It showed in her letters. They were written by installments. I could see where utter weariness of mind and body had stopped her pen; where she had recovered her strength to take it up again.

Then came the Christmas when she wrote, "I have failed so much the past year. My tasks seem heavy, and I have so little strength left. Yet I must go on. Sometimes I feel as if I could not possibly endure the hardships of another winter, for with the proverbial poverty of the hymn-writer, I cannot build a strong enough defence against the cold . . ."

I put down the letter with a cry of protest. Over me swept the old unregenerate rebellion because God had never given me, in spite of all my prayers, money to give away. The old hurt ached again in my heart. I longed to be able to give her enough for her needs, blankets for the winter, security in her old age.

For fifty years she had given her shreds of strength, her spare moments, snatched often between sunset and lamplight, to the writing of her hymns and spiritual songs, to save souls. And now, as she was reaching the end of her self-giving life, what had I to give her?

Words! I poured them out in an article for *Christian Herald*, telling about her work, now forgotten . . . and her need.

And oh, the love that poured through the mails, and emptied itself on the doorstep of that humble little mountain home!

"We just didn't know," folks explained, and of course they didn't, any more than I did before I received her first letter.

A reader who lived on a large prairie farm in Montana, twenty miles from church and post office, sent her a radio. Three generations in her family, she wrote, had sung, "I Belong to the King." She and her husband and two little sons held their own small Sunday school in their home, taking turns at being superintendent. That Sunday, the ten-year-old son had served, and had chosen "I Belong to the King" as the opening hymn. The radio came with her loving gratitude.

Amid the deluge of mail that came to me was a thrilled letter from a local missionary of the First Presbyterian Church, McKeesport, Pennsylvania. "God bless you for finding Miss Reed for me!" she wrote. She had sought for her twenty-five years ago, after reading that she lay critically ill in a Philadelphia hospital. But, to her great grief, she could neither see her nor get her address.

"Imagine my joy," Miss Florence B. Kohler wrote, "to read your article, illustrated by her picture! For years, I have had charge of several missions among young people and children of different nationalities. We try to make 'Others' our motto—and now we have the real joy of being able to do something for Miss Reed."

It would take a row of books to tell all they did, year after year! Miss Kohler's young people were a small group. The little mission, with an average, nine months of the year, of about forty, was already giving a hundred dollars a year to missions, besides its general offerings. But now it was ready to give as much again.

They loved to sing. They named their chorus for Ida L. Reed, "adopted" her, and set a little box on the piano for "love gifts" for her. "Money has never been mentioned since the day we put it there," Miss Kohler confided later, "but each week this year we have sent her at least one dollar, often two, several times five, and twice—because of generous outside gifts—ten dollars.... No more than seven of the chorus are earning money regularly. Several are young married people. But they gladly go without themselves to give to her."

What a heap of love poured out of that little box on the piano to warm a lonely old heart in West Virginia! Month after month, letters came to my desk threaded with such shining sentences as, "The lamp was a love gift. I needed it so." Or the radio batteries, the warm sweater, the spring house.

Sometimes it was the gift of laughter. They would drive out the one hundred and twenty miles to see the old hymn-writer. It took four hours each way, and often the roads gave them trouble. They came "freighted with helpfulness," and soon that small, silent homeplace in the hills was aglow with their cheer and chatter.

They would crowd around the little old organ to sing Miss Reed's own hymns to her while she played the accompaniments with feeble fingers that had drawn many a new melody from the old keys.

"It gladdens her heart," commented the understanding Miss Kohler, "to know that her hymns are not forgotten—that she is not forgotten."

Time and again, in past years, state and church organizations had proposed holding an Ida L. Reed Day, some even getting to the point of organizing; then the plans always fell through. But Miss Kohler's young people had organized an Ida L. Reed Sunday before they had known her a year! Not only in their own two missions, but in neighboring churches. They told of it so simply:

"We do not ask for anything. We just tell at both Mission Sunday Schools, morning and evening, what we are trying to do for Miss Reed's birthday. That Sunday we give the service to the singing of her hymns and the reading of some of her poems. Then members tell of their visits to Miss Reed's home, and of their impressions. We give her our offering of the day.

"In the evening the young people of the Hungarian Church also honor her at their service, and our own Ida L. Reed Chorus sings there, too, and Miss Kohler tells the story of the hymn-writer's life. These young people add their offering to ours."

That was the year a few of them took the long ride to the hills, weighted down with love gifts, a nourishing dinner, and a birthday cake ringed with candles.

"It was the happiest birthday I ever had," Miss Reed told them, her eyes starry with tears. After that, they never missed a birthday. One year, besides the usual practical gifts, they added the luxuries of two big "florist's chrysanthemums," and a birthday telegram. And, like a shining star, to top the rest, a radio surprise! Richard Maxwell had an Ida Reed hymn in his book. Miss Kohler wrote and asked him to sing it over the radio—and he did!

As I listened, in my mind's eye, I could see the silver-haired old lady to whom radio was still a miracle, sitting there in her plain little home, basking in the rare luxury of florist flowers, as "radio's slim fingers" plucked her hymn from the night and tossed it over grimy roofs and city's din to her still, snowy hills.

Did her thoughts fly back over her long ministry of music to those who were just names to most of us, but dear friends to her? To Philip Phillips, the Singing Pilgrim, for whose last hymn she wrote the words; to Ira D. Sankey, who gave her valuable guidance in her youth and who, when he, himself, was old and blind, wrote her a farewell letter . . . "We shall meet when the mists of earth are rolled away, and until that glad good morning, Good Night, Good Night!"

Did she touch spirits with the blind hymn-writer, Fanny Crosby, who found time between writing, "There's Music in the Air" and "Safe in the Arms of Jesus" to send her many loving messages; with H. P. Danks, composer of "Silver Threads Among the Gold," for whom she wrote verses when she was just a school-girl; with all those old-time hymn-writers, now in the Heavenly Choir? Were they listening, too, on her birthday night?

In spite of the separating miles, Miss Kohler's young people continued to be the kindest of neighbors. I heard much about their practical Christianity. There was a snip of gay wallpaper in the letter which read, in part, "This time they brought paper for my living room. Miss Jones does neat and fine work, papering. While she papered, Miss Welsh pasted for her. Miss Petach and Miss Zayle cleaned and polished my few pieces of furniture for the room, and together transformed it into a light, cheery place, instead of the drab one it had been so long. How I welcome the help of these blessed young people who are so quick and strong and sunny! Miss Kohler, herself, served the picnic lunch which they brought. There was nothing for me to do but rest in my chair—and thank God."

The young people cheerfully drafted their brothers and boy friends for service and carried them off to the hills to replace a cracked pane in her window, or inspect the roof for leaks. Two persuaded their husbands to travel wintry, treacherous mountain roads to mend the broken steps of her home, for fear she might trip and fall.

"She has become such a part of my life," confessed Miss Kohler, "that she is constantly in my mind. And, as for my young people, not only are they, themselves, richer for the contacts they have made with her, but our whole working together has been lifted to a higher plane."

Then came the wonder of wonders—the miracle! Even after I had heard Kate Smith announce it on the radio, and had read the Associated Press notice of it, it still seemed too good to be true.

But a humbly proud letter from Miss Reed assured me that it was so. She had received "recognition" in the form of a weekly bonus for "her substantial contribution to American music" from The American Society of Composers, Authors and Publishers.

They had not considered her humble work either naive or "corny." That great clearing house of music, organized in 1914 by Victor Herbert and several contemporaries, had examined her hymns and melodies and judged them sufficiently "worthwhile" to merit the grant. An organization, as I learned later, composed alike of such celebrities as Sergei Rachmaninoff and

Duke Ellington, Edna St. Vincent Millay and Al Johnson, Fritz Kreisler and Bing Crosby, Jascha Heifetz and Irving Berlin.

They let one of her old church friends bring that first check to her, with "a beautiful letter of appreciation," on Christmas morning, 1939. As she held it in her hands that trembled with emotion, she knew that another such check would come to her every week as long as she lived. At long last, security!

"Oh, how I wish I could have done this for you!" sighed Miss Kohler. Said the old hymn-writer, "In a way, you did. For had it not been for you and your young people, I don't think I could have possibly lived to receive it."

Miss Reed died in 1951, and lies buried in a private cemetery across the road from the Ebenezer Church, near her home. She used to wonder what would become of her precious "papers" after her death—age-yellowed files of her hymn manuscripts, penned in her careful hand-lettering, letters from other hymn-writers, composers of sacred music, publishers. They are now in the possession of the Barbour County Historical Society.

Just Eddie

The Story of Edgar A. Guest, "Poet of the People"

Edgar A. Guest was my first American friend; true, I had only met him in his "Breakfast Table Chat" in my morning newspaper, the Detroit *Free Press*, yet I clung to his column as a lost foreigner clings to the hand of one who, in a strange, new country, speaks her language.

I had left a mellow little English village, where a simple folk rich in the plain virtues, trudged placidly along, doing their duty to God and neighbor. And I had come to a great, growing American city, dynamic, swift, money-minded, where a man, it seemed, was worth what he had in dollars, where they preached a new Gospel of "Getting On." Lost and lonely, I searched desperately for my neighbor . . . my God.

I found them first in Eddie Guest's column. There, in cheery, casual verse was a neighbor's chat over the garden wall, a friend's warm, tight handclasp, a chuckle, a twinkle. He sang of familiar, friendly things, just as precious in this new country as the old—of love and laughter, home and children, friends and neighbors, dogs and daffodils — of the gain of giving, the worth of a smile, and spiritual riches — things that really mattered—tender, lilting rhymes that danced like sunbeams, or braced one for the struggle of life.

I used to wonder wistfully if I should ever meet this poet who could take a handful of words and fill them with the light of a faith that saw God in so many unexpected places.

I was to see him before I'd even had time to shed my ultra-serviceable English clothes. My accent was still so noticeable that people seldom heard what I said for listening to it.

There I stood in the lobby of the old *Free Press* building, white with fear. Hurrying people surged past me like ocean breakers over a very little pebble. I clung to a folder of my poor scraps of prose and poetry, brought here for the great man to read.

How had it all happened? Miraculously! While I was still counting my nickels as tuppence-ha' pennies, the editor of a little neighborhood newspaper had asked me to write him a weekly column. I had never done one before, but didn't I have a classic to copy? So, humbly enough, I did just that, even to starting each one with a poem.

And one day a visiting newspaperman who had noticed my columns, asked, "How'd you like to meet Eddie Guest? I know him . . ."

I was panicky at the thought. Poets had always overawed me. I trembled when he dashed up a few days later to say, "Eddie will see you at four tomorrow."

So here I was in the lobby. Little chills of fear raced up and down my spine. But I gritted my teeth and pushed my unwilling feet to the elevator—I still called it a lift—and addressed the boy in a voice high with nervousness.

"I wish to see the Poet," I announced. He stopped chewing his gum, and blinked furiously.

"The what?" he snapped.

"Mr. Edgar A. Guest, the . . ."

"Aw-w," he grinned, "just Eddie. Going up?"

Still in a daze, I went up, and out, and into an office. "Sit down," said a small, spry office boy, and went out, leaving me stranded.

I looked wildly around. Surely this was the wrong place! Every chair was full of copy paper, press clippings, and proofs. A half-emptied cup of coffee teetered on top of one pile, the remains of a sandwich on another. The desk was piled high with mail. Above it tilted a print of Lincoln, and smiling out of a silver frame at the disorder of that man's desk was a sweet-faced lady whom I afterwards learned was his wife, Nellie. Near the framed portrait was a shabby Bible, a pencil stuck in to keep the place.

I stood because there was no place to sit, until a likeable young chap, boyishly alert, came to the doorway and peered at me from under a green eyeshade.

"I have," I informed him with proper dignity, "an appointment with Mr. Edgar A. Guest, the poet."

He ran a hurried hand through coal-black hair, mussing it past hope. His shirtsleeves were rolled to his elbows; his bow tie was awry. He came in and slipped on his coat.

"I'm Eddie," he said. "Sit down." He took a chair and tilted it gently so that its contents slid to the floor. He did it so expertly I knew he'd learned how through constant practice. Then he swept the contents off another, and motioned me to be seated. I dropped helplessly into it as he appropriated the other. He didn't sit in his. He rode it, like a charger, facing and gripping its back.

"Now!" he began, grinning that engaging grin of his.

I sat there, stunned and silent. So this was the Poet! I had met other poets in England, for my sister liked them. They had drifted, dreamy-eyed and velvet-coated, in a world of their own. When they talked, nobody expected to understand them. Their hair was long, and their ties soft and flowing. They had what my sister called an aura . . . not a bow tie, a whiff of printer's ink, a twinkle!

"Well," said the brisk young man astride the chair, looking as if he didn't know what it was to drift.

Furtively I produced my poems, my bits of prose. "Mr. Campbell," I stammered, "s-said I could s-show you these. I wrote them."

In a flash the brisk young man became the neighbor, the friend of his column. He seemed to light up from within, to radiate an actual warmth—a sort of soul-sunniness that shone all around in that cluttered office, and made it a grand place to be. One warmed one's self in the friendliness, the kindness, the understanding of him, as at a fire on a cold day.

A hundred things, I knew, clamored for his attention in the press room, but he had time for me. There he sat, carefully reading every word of my handwritten copy. No skimming, no glossing over, his entire attention riveted on those pages, as though they really mattered.

Then he began to talk to me—as if I, too, mattered. I found myself talking to him, all fear and shyness gone, as if I had known him all my life. And how he listened! Every once in awhile he would give a quick little nod of his head that said, "Yes, yes. I understand."

Then as I finally rose to go, he patted my shoulder, "Go on writing," he told me, his eyes stilling to a swift, direct earnestness. "I think you have something to give folks."

Not a word about what I could get by writing — but what I could give!

I came home with some of his radiance shining within me. I had thought that to be an American I must be a go-getter. Now I knew better. I could be a go-giver, like Eddie Guest. Gone was the chill of fear, the fog of doubt. In their place was something this royal giver had given me—courage, faith in my own dream, the start of my life's work!

That had all happened twenty years ago. And now, here I was on my way to see him again, to get his story for a magazine. As the taxi sped by spurts through Detroit's congested streets I thought of the success that had come to him since I saw him last. Now he was a national figure. He had a dozen books of verse to his credit, almost as many of prose. For years he had been writing a poem a day, with hundreds of papers carrying his syndicated verse. It was estimated that he had a million readers.

Moreover, he had lectured on platforms throughout America, sometimes receiving as much as a thousand dollars for an evening's program of his poems and humorous stories; sometimes just a heartfelt, "Thanks, Eddie," from the church or welfare group which had solicited his talent to help raise money for a worthy cause.

Then, for years, he had been a radio personality, with every loyal fan feeling he had found a lifelong friend in Eddie.

The big city roared around me. Humanity ebbed and flowed like a seething sea. Police and crooks fought it out under our very wheels. My taxi driver added his oaths to the traffic snarl, while a fire siren tore the air.

This was no small Main Street. On every side lurked the sordid and sodden, the sardonic and sinful. For forty years, I mused, Eddie Guest had bucked all this—yet not a vestige showed in his verse.

As the taxi sped recklessly on, I thought back over the years; of all the things that had happened that could have changed a lesser man than Eddie—the war, the depression, the hectic years when so many Americans mistook jazz for joy. Yet he had gone serenely on writing about the American home as it used to be before it was just a place to hang your hat, or a dull hole from which to go places and see things.

And even when our Sweet Land of Liberty had gone on its final jag, and had grown hilariously hiccuppy, the family table was still to him the place at which to ask a blessing, never the place to drink yourself under. He still thought in terms of cookie jars instead of gin fizzes.

Eddie had never changed his tune to suit the times. When all the world was debunking, he went on extolling the scoffed-at virtues, caroling the old faith, untouched by the ironic barb of the ultra-modern, the amused disdain of the intellectual, the academic wrangle as to whether he were a second Riley or a mere jingler.

The taxi, spurning the old place, stopped at the immense new *Free Press* building. A suave, sleek attendant, instead of the brash little boy of other days, took me up to the fourth floor. I passed light, orderly offices where girls clipped and sorted. Then I came to the one I sought. A man, his back to me, was dictating to his secretary.

Quickly the dictating stopped. Out flashed a friendly hand. Same old engulfing handclasp! I looked up . . . same twinkle . . . same mouth, humorous and sad at the same time. Same neighborly warmth sunning the place. I came a little nearer, half expecting him to pat my shoulder.

He invited me into the inner office, evidently his own retreat. I looked around that shining, well-kept room, searching for something that reminded me of the old one. The print of Abe Lincoln, dog-eared and warped, was gone—but there he was on the desk, done in bronze. A more recent portrait of the sweet-faced lady was there; beside it, a vase of garden flowers. And he had a new Bible—with a pencil still holding the place!

"Have a seat," said he. He rode his, just as he did twenty years ago, his arms and busy hands across the back. The passing years had brought a few Lincoln-esque furrows to his face, where humor lurked and the marks of old griefs. He was a bit heavier, and his hair was frosted with a sprinkling of iron-grey. But the buoyant boyishness was still there. His bow tie was still awry. No, fame hadn't done a thing to him. He was still "just Eddie."

"Well?" he said, and grinned at me.

"I want to know," I said, "how you came to be a poet."

"But I'm not!" he protested. "I'm a reporter. That's all I do—report, in rhyme. Well, here's the story."

I can't tell it as he did. But, in substance, this is it.

Almost any Sunday around the year 1888, you might have met a little lad trudging the hills around Birmingham, England, with his tall, wise dad—who liked folks—who said it was character that made a man, not class or clothes—who told about truly fine people he knew—not fairy princes or fighting giants, but "just folks," like the people who lived on your street. And as that little fellow, Eddie Guest, listened he absorbed many a truth that in later years he wove into a bright new verse.

Those walks and talks continued after business reverses in England had brought the family—father, mother and five children—to America in 1891 to start anew. Only now it was about this great new land of opportunity that Dad talked.

"It's the greatest country on earth," he'd say. "Under this flag you can become anything you wish, if you have the strength and the ability and the will to persevere. I wish I had come sooner, Sonny."

It was tough going for the little family. The panic of 1892 swept Dad into the ranks of the unemployed. They knew privation and anxiety, but together they weathered the storm. Young Eddie got a job for after school and Saturdays in the corner drug store.

There he met a man who started him up the ladder from office boy to columnist. He was one of a group of men, all regular customers. Eddie liked him especially, partly because he was a bookkeeper, like Dad, but mostly because he called him by his name. Not, "Hi, boy!" but, "Here, Eddie."

One day Eddie was sent on an errand to the old *Free Press* building, and there ran head on into his drug store friend.

"'Lo, Eddie!" he greeted him. "How'd you like to work here?"

He may have been joking. But fourteen-year-old Eddie took it as a serious offer, and that summer, when school was out, he went to the *Free Press* as boy-of-all-work in the bookkeeping department, where, at first, his "figuring" consisted of marking up the baseball scores on the bulletin board in front of the building, for which he received a salary of a dollar and a half a week. But he was on the *Free Press* payroll, to stay there all his life!

However, the active Eddie didn't like bookkeeping. He was interested in folks, not figures. He longed to be on the editorial floor, where news was, where men dashed in and out, after a big story, with a grand scoop. That was the job! Not sitting still on a tall stool, fooling with figures.

Still he toughed it through for a couple of years. Things were darker than ever at home, with his dad sick unto death. Even his boss, the friendly bookkeeper, was away on vacation. Restlessness sizzled inside him, ran over.

Young Eddie marched upstairs and asked the acting editor-in-chief if he could find a place for him on the editorial floor. The veteran chief offered the youngster the job of pressroom office boy. Eddie accepted with alacrity. He was now sixteen, and that year his father died.

In the years that followed, Eddie, who wanted to see life, was to see it at its grimmest—as a reporter on the police beat. Murders, suicides, assaults, robberies, the whole cycle of casualty and crime.

"That sort of work," said Eddie, "does one of two things to a fellow. I've seen it do both. It either fills him with bitterness or pity."

Then came a new job. He was made assistant to the exchange editor, where he clipped fillers from newspapers that came from all over the country. Much of what he clipped and pasted was verse. Sometimes he would say to the snipping scissors, "I believe I could write a poem like that."

One day he tried it. He wrote a poem in Negro dialect and slipped it under the office door of the Sunday editor. It was pretty crude, admitted Eddie, but perhaps that blessed editor saw promise in it. For he not only printed it, but gave Eddie his first proper by-line. That humble little poem opened the Sunday page to Eddie—the lowly forerunner of thousands of inspiring poems yet to come.

Soon this clipping from other writers' columns began to pall. He wanted to do a column of his own.

"No," said the chief, "you're too young. You're doing fine. Just hold steady. Don't strain yourself!" But Eddie's harping on that one string made the chief so column-conscious that one day, in sheer desperation, he up and bought one! "That," laughed Eddie, "was a blow to me. But the imported column didn't last long, and soon they told me I could try one. Say, was that a happy day!"

Gleefully, Eddie got busy. He called his weekly column "Blue Monday," and started each off with an original "home rhyme." And it was in this simple verse that he showed his particular kind of genius. He sang of his home, his Nellie, little domestic doings; of counting his wealth in friends and good neighbors; of finding God in a garden. Not great poems, heavy with profound thought or deep with abstruce utterances, but just simple verses, touched with that divine thing we call humanness.

When Nell did up the pickles, or lost her pocket-book for the umteenth time, or fell an easy prey to the glib tongue of a doorstep salesman, or was panic-stricken without him when it thundered; or when their Boston pup tore the curtains, the baby cut a tooth, or son, Bud, the rascal, caught the measles, Eddie told his column readers all about it in gently-joshing verse.

Soon his weekly column became a daily, under the title of "Breakfast Table Chat," and his poems were being clipped and printed by papers far and wide. From there, it was but a step to the publication of his first collection, "Home Rhymes — Done into a Book by Harry R. Guest, in the Year Nineteen Hundred and Nine, at Detroit."

It was the work of Harry Guest, the printer, for Eddie Guest, the poet. Brother Harry set that first little book by hand, in the attic of his home. He had only enough type to set eight pages at a time. When those pages were printed, the forms were broken up, and eight more set. The book ran to 136 pages, and 800 copies were printed in this laborious fashion.

Two years later, Harry brought out Eddie's second book of poems, "Just Glad Things," using the same slow method, working in the same attic, but this time, he printed 1,500 copies. And two years after that, he launched the third book of Eddie's poems, named "Breakfast Table Chat," after his column, this time in monotype, with a breathtaking 3,500 copies.

By that time Fame was stalking Eddie. He could have sold his next book, "A Heap o' Livin'," to not one but three publishers. Reilly & Lee of Chicago published it in 1916. Its sensational success bewildered Eddie—and his publishers! Ten years after publication it was still a best seller. Half a million copies had been sold, and in later years, over a million.

"And that," said Eddie, "is how I came to be a rhyming reporter."

The telephone bell had been ringing constantly, and now that patient peach of a secretary, who had murmured soothing replies to callers for almost two hours, had questions that must be answered. Could a lecture date be arranged? Mr. So-and-So was in the city to interview Mr. Guest for Such-and-Such magazine, and when and where could he meet him? An author and publication of such importance that I shot an awed look at Eddie. His brow was knit over the typed reply to a fan letter, one of a great stack brought in for signing.

I caught his concentrated eye. "She wants me," he worried, "to quote for her one of my favorite poems, and I can't think of a line I ever wrote."

But I could! "I have harvested much from my acres of life." Before I could voice the line, two others rushed in, demanding my attention:

"The golden threads in the warp of life
Are the sorrow-tugs at your heart."

Then I was left alone while Eddie busied himself with things he must do before kindly driving me home. I sat there, dreaming. Yes, it was the tears with the smiles that had given his poems their rainbow gleam of hope. The "sorrow-tugs"—how well I knew them!

The death of their first baby, Eddie's little girl. Only thirteen months old. Waving a merry farewell to him in the morning . . . dead before midnight.

The shock of it had stunned the city. Women who knew Eddie only through his column wept on their own doorsteps, in street cars. In shop and factory, tenement and mansion, there were eyes that could see nothing but the little wisp of crepe on Eddie's door.

The bereaved young father went bravely on writing his poems, but now there was a new compassion underlying the humor. A shining thread, spun from sorrow, gleamed in the homespun. And Nellie? She laid empty arms on the empty crib, and sobbed, "I must have another little girl!" So they adopted one, three years old and homeless, to fill the vast emptiness of their small flat.

After that, it was small Marjorie who inspired some of Eddie's best poems. Column readers saw her in her first new bonnet; heard her lisp her evening prayer; shared Eddie's chagrin when she spurned his extravagant new Christmas doll for her old rag baby.

But a rented second-story flat was no place for a lively little girl. They needed a yard for her to romp in, a garden, and—Eddie said it with bated breath—a home of their own for the child. Because a kindly banker was willing to lend Eddie the money for the down payment, the house was soon theirs.

"If ever a couple found real happiness," said Eddie, "we found it under the roof of that Leicester Court house."

It was here that Eddie discovered the joys and woes of gardening, recording them in some of his most appealing verses. It was here their own baby son was born—the rascally Bud who grew up in the column. It was here that he signed those important contracts for the syndicating of his poems, and the publication of his record-breaking book, "A Heap o' Livin'."

Then came years of grief—the long fight for little Marjorie's life. For three months they battled the black shadow of death while she wasted away with typhoid fever. Then, mercifully, the fever broke, and the wan, weary child began her slow convalescence. They dared to be happy again.

But not for long. That summer, it was scarlet fever they fought. Bud was sent away to the country and his dad banished from the house. He could only see his Nellie and Marjorie now from outside the window. He poured it all out in "Homesick," and in homes all over the land there were other fathers who kept anxious watch with "the dad beside the gateway of the home he can't go in."

They conquered scarlet fever only to find a worse foe attacking the child's weakened system—tuberculosis! Was there any chance to save her?

The doctors advised a home in the country air, where Marjorie could live in the open, sleep on a sun-drenched, breeze-swept porch. With a heavy heart, Eddie set about selling that beloved first real home of theirs, with all its rich associations, its dear memories. He wanted to take with him every finger mark, every hammer dent, the wallpaper where Bud had scrawled those pencil marks. "I've treasured them for years," grieved Eddie. "They were the first he ever wrote."

They found the new home for Marjorie. It was a noble Georgian residence beside a golf fairway, over which the air swept clean and sweet, and full of healing for sick lungs. It had sunny spaciousness where an exploring wheelchair could roll when Marjorie grew better.

But the price! The unscalable mountain of the down payment required! Seventy-five hundred dollars, the rest to be covered by a mortgage. Where could they get the money? Where find the securities?

And again, Eddie had a friend—"rich but generous." He went to this friend with his burden of grief— this poet-father who had lifted the load of thousands— and the rich man surely laid up treasure in heaven that day, for he handed Eddie a check for the full amount, "with not a scratch of paper" between them!

So into the lovely home the Guest family moved, and here Janet, their own little daughter, was born.

Eddie was soon singing songs about the new home, weaving iridescent dreams into the fabric of the curtains; mellowing unweathered walls with his magic touch of whimsical humor and gentle laughter.

Then one day when the air was full of birds and butterflies and promise, Marjorie slipped away. The little girl who had danced into their grief-stricken lives, and brought them from the rented flat to their own palatial mansion had gone on, perhaps to find a lovelier home for them wherever heaven is.

I came out of my reverie to hear Eddie saying he was ready to start home. As we whizzed along in his smart little car, he talked wistfully of his little mother, who had so wanted him to be a minister . . . in whose memory he had for years taken the pulpit on Mother's

Day. And of his gallant father who had so wanted to live long enough to help give Eddie a college education.

I wanted to tell him that surely the little mother was proud now of the blessed ministry of her poet-preacher who spoke from press pulpits the country over. And that surely his father now knew that he'd given his boy something far more precious than a college degree—the wisdom of an understanding heart.

But we reached my home before a single word would come round the lump in my throat.

The article was written and published, and Eddie wired me to say how much he liked it. Then I traveled a lot, keeping in touch with him through letters from Detroiters, press clippings, newscasts, and numerous magazine articles about him.

In 1935 he was in Hollywood receiving $3,500 a week, and living with his family in a fabulous home there, rented from a movie star. He stood that way of life for only three frustrating months, then he shook the gold dust of Hollywood from off his shoes, and returned to his home city. He said he felt better earning his salary!

In 1942, a longhand copy of his poem, "America," was sold for fifty thousand dollars to one of his friends, the money going to Uncle Sam who gave war bonds in exchange.

In 1945, his beloved Nellie died. From the day he had first met her at a friend's wedding, where she was the bridesmaid and he the best man, he had loved her, and after a whirlwind courtship of two months, had married her. For forty years she had been heart of his heart, in sunshine and shadow. And now he was alone!

There followed a series of the most heart-wringing poems in all Eddie's long career as a columnist. They were his letters to Nellie, written as if she were merely away on a visit, and not in the Great Beyond. In them, he told her of things at home, about Bud and Janet, and their children; about neighborhood happenings; about how he missed her.

He was easing the agony of loneliness in his own heart in the best way he knew. But, in doing so, he was also easing the heavy grief of thousands, for that was the year when World War II ended, and throughout the land there were mourners for the newly-dead. Letters poured in to thank Eddie for those poems that came from a broken heart, and perhaps they comforted him a little, for he always wanted to help anyone in trouble.

In 1951, 69-year-old Eddie was starring daily on NBC's "A Guest In Your Home," and charming television viewers with his "suave platform manner, nimble eyebrows, and vibrant voice that radiates sincerity."

Then came his 70th birthday with honors galore. Ever since 1936, Detroit's mayors and Michigan's governors had been proclaiming "Eddie Guest Days," but for this gala occasion they pulled out all the stops! The Michigan House and Senate paused to take note of the occasion in an appreciative joint resolution. The Michigan Legislature passed a resolution designating Eddie Guest as the state's poet laureate. John S. Knight, editor and publisher of the *Free Press*, commissioned a foremost portrait painter to do a portrait of this native son who had grown up with Detroit.

During the past thirty years of being a beloved national figure, Eddie had already accumulated a rare collection of various honors—"the academic, the civic, the homespun, the odd." He held two honorary doctorates, was a Kentucky colonel, an honorary citizen of the State of Texas, the poet laureate of the fishermen, a chief by adoption in Oklahoma's Otoe tribe of Indians, in 1938 was awarded the Poor Richard Silver Medal of achievement by Philadelphia's Poor Richard Club, and had a chrysanthemum and a school named for him!

On his 70th birthday, Eddie was trim, brisk, erect, natty, still writing his daily poem, proud that he had never missed a deadline.

In the years that followed came disquieting news. Eddie's eyesight was failing, although he was still able to write a poem a day by peering at his typewriter and copy through a powerful reading glass which he had suspended by a tripod arrangement. He had given up playing golf because he could not see. No more holes-in-one!

Then came news of an operation, and a long convalescence, and that he no longer went to the Detroit Golf Club for dinner. It embarrassed him not to be able to see people clearly and to identify them readily.

Eddie had once told me that he hoped he would be still working on the *Free Press* until Death wrote "30" after his last line of copy.

Instead, he died quietly and peacefully in his sleep, fifteen days short of his 79th birthday. There was no sadness of farewell, no last words. He just rolled over in his sleep, and was gone.

When I heard the news, I took down my well-thumbed copy of his "Collected Verse." He had autographed it for me in 1934, writing on the title page, "Here are my best wishes for your success." I opened it at random and my eyes fell on the verse:

And yet the cares are many and the
  hours of toil are few:
There is not time enough on earth for
  all I'd like to do:
But, having lived and having toiled, I'd
  like the world to find
Some little touch of beauty that my
  soul had left behind.

Grace Noll Crowell
The Poet and the Woman

"I glittered it!" The glad cry rang through an old rambling farmhouse in Iowa, and with it an absorbed little girl began to be a poet!

She had been playing with a pewter tea-set which belonged to an older sister. Busy baby hands had dried the toy cups and plates, and never were little dishes dried so thoroughly, rubbed so hard.

Then it happened! The rubbing jerked to an amazed stop. Little Grace stared, breathless and unbelieving, at the small gray teapot in her hand. Wonderingly she lifted it to the window. It shone like silver in the sun! Her startled, round-eyed gaze went from the shining teapot to the dull pieces on the tray. Then, as the truth dawned on her, the wonder of it shone in her heart, glowed in her dark eyes. No fairy wand—just a dust-cloth and long, loving rubbing until her arms ached. That had made it shine!

Tenderly she gathered every dull little piece into her lap to rock and croon over. "I'll glitter you," she promised them. "I'll make you silver in the sun."

Soon the little girl of the pewter teapot and her family moved in closer to town, to a plain, simple farmhouse set down in apple and plum orchards. "There was much work to be done," she told me, "and I did my share of it. But somehow the tasks, in the light of the years, reflect the glory of scented clover, red berries, ripening apples, and the heady wine of youth. Oh, the scarlet currants, the glistening blackberries, the clean, clear green of gooseberries, and the purple clusters of vineyard grapes!"

And across the road from the orchard home was an evergreen grove, the joy of that little girl's heart. Here she "kept house" under the trees, raking the pine needles into squares for rooms, setting her woodsy table with fir-cone dishes, discovering a dream world.

But here the poet began to possess the housewife. There was deep content in the little dishes — but a strange, sweet disturbance when the sun slanted through the tree tops and cast a mesh of gold about her restless little feet. The small child, in her pine-needle playhouse, knew no reason for the yearning ache that swept through her at such times. She knew no reason why wet lilacs, a bird's plaintive cry in the dusk, a crimson sunset, should stir something within her like a flame, a cry, a song . . . like feeble wings spreading.

Nor did her family—dear prosaic household, busy with the urgent duties of a well-kept farm. So, when, at eight, she read them her first poem, they turned puzzled eyes on her to listen—and then they laughed!

Little Grace had turned poet! Well, well! Another

indulgent laugh, and then they resumed their talk about ploughing and planting—things that mattered. Poetry didn't.

But it mattered—terribly—to the little girl choking back her tears. It mattered more than anything else in her world that she had seen such a sunset and tried, since she had no brushes, to paint it in words. She had been standing, one bleak November twilight, at a western window, looking out across the cornfields, the shocks all darkened by the oncoming night. The cattle had been turned in to forage, and the cold wind whined through the dry, shivering husks. Over the low, wide land a black night was crouching. To a little girl who loved shining things—who would one day name her books *Flame in the Wind, Silver in the Sun, White Fire, Light of the Years, This Golden Summit, The Radiant Quest, The Lifted Lamp, Splendor Ahead, Some Brighter Dawn*— there was something foreboding and eerie in the ever-deepening dusk.

Then her eye caught that for which it was always searching—a gleam! Low on the horizon, there it was, a thin, crimson line, left by the setting sun! It was night . . . and still not night, for the sun's red line was there. It was day . . . and yet, against the high white light of noon, it was in reality night!

Baffled, as is every poet, in a desperate, futile striving to capture the uncapturable, she wrote in childish scrawl:

> The night was dark,
> And the sun shone red as fire—

There were other lines equally at odds, but that was

enough for a practical family. With burning cheeks a crushed little girl, her heart aching, crept upstairs to put away her pad and pencil.

She was married, with a baby son of her own, before she took them up again—as sadly as ever she had hidden them away. What had happened in the meantime?

School, college, music, courtship, marriage. She had met Norman H. Crowell when she was twenty. He was "different." When he was not working in the bank he wrote articles—a dazzling thing to a dreamy-eyed girl who had once tried to write a poem! Moreover, editors printed what he wrote in newspapers and magazines. Wonderful!

Married, they moved to a little valley town twenty miles south of the old homestead. Norman recalled, with a characteristic chuckle, that first little honeymoon home.

"We had gone to Des Moines on a wedding trip, and bought a complete outfit of furniture for the fabulous sum of two hundred and forty-eight dollars and thirty-one cents. I still have the original bill. They tossed in a wire kettle-cleaner to clinch the bargain. The carpets were nothing but a good quality of burlap on which somebody had spilled ink. But they looked like Wilton velvet to your Uncle Norm!"

Grace smiled at this man who made it a point of honor to laugh at life; to clown not only in print and on the platform, but in the home. "Norman," she confided once, "is the one man in all the world who could so marvelously have understood me and so completely have lived for me and my happiness. Isn't it wonderful for me to have had him?"

"I was the good provider," he chortled. "I had laid in twelve quarts of plums, canned by my landlady. Day after day little Gracie would gaze at that row of red plums on the top shelf in the kitchen and rhapsodize. She always loved the look of canned fruit . . . When we finally opened the cans, they hadn't been sweetened at all. Not a pinch of sugar ever saw them! Was I mad?"

Burlap carpets, sour plums . . . but also a wire kettle cleaner in the loving, busy hands of the little girl of the pewter teapot. Eagerly she told me about it. "It glittered—that new little honeymoon home. It could have been one of the heavenly mansions let down just for me. True, it had a sulky stove that would not draw, and a splintery-floored kitchen that made scrubbing difficult. But it had gleaming windows looking west and east. My dishes were shining on the shelves. My plated silverware glistened in its drawer. Sheets and pillow cases were in their ordered places, and I would put on a crimson tea gown when my neighbors came to tea—" And then in a delighted aside, "I have always had such friendly neighbors!" As if anyone needed to be told that!

Three perfect years of sweet memories preserved in some of the tenderest of her domestic poems of a later day. Each morn she rose "to meet the day with wings upon her feet." Each night she paused, remembering "some gay, adventurous lovely thing." Again a deep content had come to her in this bigger woodsy play-house. The flame, the cry, the bursting song, the

beating wings seemed to have fled her heart, leaving it
   ... like a still, brown nest,
Where little soft, warm baby things
May snuggle down to rest.

How she loved transforming that new little house into a home, keeping a shining kitchen, being a thrifty little manager, a good wife! Racing along with the joyous months, breathlessly busy, until finally there was a radiant new reason to sing and dream—baby clothes to make. Now she must learn to be a perfect mother!

But with the longed-for little son came disaster—a nerve and spine weakness that stayed. Barely had they reached their second home under the elms of a friendly small village in Minnesota before the young mother's health failed entirely. For weary months she lay ... waiting for pain to cease, for sleep to come, for strength to revive, for a gleam. Every fiber of her ached to be moving swiftly about her business of homemaking and mothering. The helplessness of a baby son cried to her; the needs of the dear small home. There was nothing she could do anymore but bear pain patiently ... and be still ... and wait.

Grace had never been very good at keeping still or waiting. But there in her school of suffering she "minded the Master" and learned of Him. Learned how to carry a cross and lift another's; how to be "Brave for Life." Learned, in her sudden loss of them, the beauty and glory of everyday things—the lilies of the field, the sparrows, blue-and-white dishes, a little home.

Some of her later poems about that little home, because of her illness grown so sad and still, hold the

crooning note of a lullaby; as though she would rock it
in her arms, along with the baby son—that motherless
small house that had to muddle along without her.

As the months crept by on leaden feet, the suffering
young mother braced herself to face a life of invalidism. Over her brief bright day there seemed now a
black night crouching. Her eyes, heavy for lack of
sleep, searched the horizon for a gleam . . . Suddenly
there flashed into her consciousness the memory of
that crimson line . . . when it was night and yet not
night! That little-girl poem. Oh, if only she could write!
Then, even if she should never be strong again, she
could help.

The memory of old "well" days stabbed her. The
way the little house used to glitter. The primrose on
the sill, the braided rugs, the singing, shining teakettle,
the savor of her fresh-baked bread. The sound of dear
home-coming steps and her heart hurrying with her to
light a flame, singing with the happy kettle. Then the
ache in her throat, the flooding of her eyes

> With an ancient tenderness—
> The old, old sweetness of service
> For a man
> Who looks at me from the doorway
> As if he were glad.

Even in her sick depression she knew he would
always be glad when he neared any threshold where
she was. But she—O dear God, could she ever be recon-
ciled to not doing her share . . . to being a burden?
If she could write!

Thus with the faith of a great and simple soul, she

prayed to be a poet. Earnestly she poured it all out—
her utter inability to write verse; her need to know
how; her solemn pledge never to write anything un-
worthy of the source of her inspiration . . . When her
husband found her picking at his typewriter with two
uncertain fingers, he laughed affectionately, rumpled
her dark hair, and pocketed the poem. He was the
writer in that family. Her job was to get rosy and
strong again.

She wrote another poem about night and a broken
home, a maimed mother, a mourning mate. Just a nest
left cold and desolate, but the thought of it wrung a
heart that was ever "a comrade to the birds of the air."
She called it "The Marshland," and her pen painted
the picture. Night coming down on the low marshland,
a star peering out of the western sky; and floating down
from the darkening heights the plaintive honk of a
wild bird's cry.

> No answering call from his nesting mate,
> From water or rushes or wet dark loam,
> And silhouetted against the sky
> A lonely hunter is going . . . home.

Her husband admitted that it was fair. To satisfy
her, he sent it off to a magazine. It was immediately accepted! Since that happy day she has sold many thousands of her poems to leading magazines in this country and wherever English is spoken, and has twenty-
two books of poetry to her credit, also eight children's
books, and six devotional books. But no acceptance has
so thrilled her as did that first one by the editor of
The Outing Magazine.

"Norman brought the acceptance from the little

northern post office," she told me. "I can see it all, the sunlight in the tiny room, my baby with his blocks, and I dragging about at some little task . . . He handed me the letter, and I sat down flat on the floor and hugged it. The check was for only five dollars, but it looked bigger than fifty to me!"

"Did you buy anything with it?"

"Did I? I always called that linen tablecloth my Marshland one. And after that, each little thing that I bought to shine and glisten in my small rooms was named in my mind for the poem that put it there . . . It was a comfort, in those young days, to do this for my home. It made up, in a way, for all that I couldn't . . ."

One hears the catch in her pleasant voice, and is sorry. For although there is nothing organically wrong, poor health has sent her back to a sick bed time and again. Repeatedly through the years she has had to run her house by "remote control" while flat on her back. And there have been "desert stretches" of greater suffering when it must be left to the devoted hands of helpers.

But between these occasional set-backs, she was well enough for many years to appear on concert and radio programs.

"I went along," grinned Norman, "to carry the aspirin and lead the applause."

When I asked Grace Noll Crowell, away back in 1933, if I might write my first article about her for *Christian Herald* readers, she begged, "Deal gently with me and my simple work. Above all, don't represent me as smug, will you? As one who is constantly going

about telling the sad old world to smile—and smile—
and smile? I couldn't bear that. I am not brave one bit.
I am not strong. But because I have suffered and have
been afraid, and because I have 'waited through the
dark'—simply because there was nothing else to do—
I have tried earnestly and prayerfully to give out something that I, myself, got there in the dark, and always
it has been God . . . I wrote a poem recently and called
it 'All Suffering Is Lonely.' In my verse I try to make
it less lonely, that's all; to remind my readers that God
knows and understands."

Many of her finest poems have come out of the
weary hours of illness—the famous "Wait," "A Prayer
for Courage," and "This, Too, Will Pass"—poems that
have flown into countless sick rooms with comfort and
healing in their wings. Collected into a little book
called *Songs for Courage,* in 1937, they were oftener
under the pillows of a hospital bed than between book
ends. Doctors wrote of their being passed from hand to
hand along the friendly wards of suffering until they
literally fell to pieces; of their being carried to the very
threshold of heaven on the whisper of the dying.

> Wait . . .
> I have learned God never will forget
> To light His lamp. If we but wait for it
> It will be lit.

It is wise for a poet with a journalist husband to
look philosophically on house-moving. Grace can remember six of them, and writes:

> As long ago I learned
> Home may be near,
> Home may be far—

But it is anywhere where Love
And a few plain household treasures are.

There was the honeymoon home, and that home in
a quaint little Minnesota village where her health
broke. Then they moved back into the home state
where Reid, the second son, was born. He is now both
an artist and a poet, living at present in his mother's
home, trying, since Norman's death, to be her strong
right arm. "I could not manage without him," sighed
Grace.

Their next home was in Sioux City, under the
eaves of the college, a step from the campus. Here the
neighbors were faculty members, and wonderfully
kind to a shy young mother who wrote poems in her
spare time. They invited her to read them at one of
their meetings. She was so scared she almost fainted.

"You recited with such feeling, my dear," one of
the learned listeners told her. Grace smiled a grateful,
wan smile, knowing how barely that "feeling" had es-
caped being the hysterical sobbing of stage fright.

It was here they bought their first car, and Grace,
in a linen duster and floating motor veil, rode forth to
scale the heights of the hills known as the Broken Kettle. The very name intrigued the little girl of the pewter
teapot. Coming upon them in the early dusk of an
autumn day, they gave her a poem. It sang in her head,
clear through to the last line.

"I sold that poem to *Scribner's Magazine*," she said,
"and I all but died of joy. I remember getting the check
on Monday morning. How that washing ever got done
I don't know! I had been placing material with many

of the smaller magazines, but to reach such heights was almost more than I had dared to hope!"

Their third son, Norton, was also born here in the shadow of the college. He is the "intellectual" of the family, being graduated with honors from the full college course in three years. Then with his Ph.D. from Harvard, and a year's scholarship at the Sorbonne, he entered his chosen field of service and is now teaching in the University of New Mexico.

Then came the important move, in 1917, to Texas! Home at last! To root in the red soil of the South, her mother's land. She tells of it in "Heritage":

> My mother bore me—looking toward the South,
> A fierce nostalgia clutching at her heart.
> My father, stoic product of the North,
> Could never understand, nor have a part
> In her wild longing for the languid South;
> But hidden in my veins she left to me
> A smouldering passion for white Southern
>   moons
> And soft warm winds that sweep up from
>   the sea.
> And after years of wandering—I have found
> Her land at last.

They welcomed her with something more than typical Southern hospitality. They loved her on sight. They heaped honors on her, prizes. They not only trod a neighborly path to her door, but they invited all America to tread it with them! And in the years that followed, a good part of America did—in spirit. Not only by mail. Along the radio airways thousands of women traveled to knock on her door.

Ted Malone, after reading one of her poems on his "Between the Book-ends" programs, wrote her, "You might be interested in knowing that I have had several hundred copies of that poem sent in to me by folks who wanted to hear it read." Which certainly did interest her; for people, in the last few months, had already bought thirty-six thousand cards bearing the same poem!

Another broadcaster quoted a Grace Noll Crowell poem on his program, and when crediting it said that the poet's home was in Texas, although he didn't know just where. But his listeners did. Letters poured in from every state in the Union to tell him that Grace lives at 719 Lowell Street, Dallas. Some, for good measure, told him her birthday. "America," he wrote her, "certainly knows where you live."

Yes, recognition came swiftly to the little girl of the pewter teapot when she came home to Texas. And, appropriately enough, homes figured in every step of the way—and neighbors! She loves to tell how she was "discovered" by a neighbor while she was still living in Wichita Falls. That dear soul found out that the new lady next door wrote poems. She read a few—was enchanted. She ran to tell another neighbor. "She writes the most beautiful things. Just think! A real poet—living on our street!"

So they gave a tea, and asked Grace to come and read some of her verse. "I nearly died again," she confessed. "I trembled all over. My teeth chattered so that I could hardly speak at all. I managed to get through the first poem, and the second, then broke down on the third and actually cried! I was so discouraged I said I would never attempt to lift my voice in public again."

"But you did!"

"Only because of their understanding and inspiration. They kept encouraging me, bless them, until I finally found out that people, in the main, are kind and not critical at all; and if I do my best I have nothing to fear. That was twenty years ago, but those loyal women, organized into the Crowell Circle, still meet regularly to read my poems, although hundreds of miles away from the new neighbors they so lovingly sponsored. And, oh, what was destined to grow from that first Texas tea party!"

It was in a neighbor's home that another great step was made. The Crowells had moved to their Dallas home, and again it was a tea. This time the guest of honor was an Englishwoman. She was quiet and charming, easy to entertain, and doubtless Grace—who had grown accustomed to reading her poems by now—did her friendly best for the neighborhood stranger.

Before she left, the cultured young woman called on Grace and gravely asked if she might be allowed to introduce her poems to the English magazines. She was the head of one of England's largest literary agencies. "It was like a fairy tale," glowed Grace. For so well did the quiet visitor do her work that soon Britishers were regarding Grace as their very own, so that I received from my English sister a clipping of "Someone Had Prayed," with a penciled note, reading, "A beautiful thing written by one of our best-loved English poets, Grace Noll Crowell."

And then a stupendous surprise! The editor of *Holland's*, to whom she had been sending occasional poems, wrote her an encouraging letter, telling her that he felt she had something to say to America's "millions of little homes," especially to the mothers who kept them. He also felt, he said, that she could, if she wished, become a nationally—perhaps internationally—known poet. This from an editor, not from an indulgent neighbor or friend!

Norman read the letter in silence. Until then he had insisted that he was the writer in the family. Now he insisted no longer. With casual cheerfulness he subordinated his career to hers, and from that time on devoted himself to her work.

"You see, it was this way," he grinned. "The greatest handicap a writing-man can possibly have is another writer in the same family who can outwrite him. Here I would spend the better part of a day pounding a thing that netted me a mere pittance—when properly revised. And she would flit into a room, like a butterfly, flop onto the old machine and thump out a poem that knocks somebody for fifty dollars! There ought to be a law—"

All of which nonsense didn't fool Grace one bit. "Norman," she said, her eyes suddenly misting, "is a very gallant gentleman."

In one of his rare serious moments he explained, "There isn't room in our sort of home for two careers —and this poetry business means so much to Grace."

With a capable husband to take care of the mechanics of writing, she could give more time to creative work. It was no longer a spare-time job. It was a full-time profession. Her poems now began to appear regularly in the leading magazines of America and England. The Poetry Society of Texas awarded her first prize for her first collection of verse, "White Fire," published in 1925. Besides an edition brought out in England, it was done in Braille. "Silver in the Sun" was published three years later; "Miss Humpety Comes to Tea" the following year. "Flame in the Wind" and "Songs of Courage" after that. And then "Light of the Years" and "Bright Destiny," followed by "This Golden Summit," "Songs of Hope," "Songs of Faith," "Songs for Courage," and a long procession of others, published by Harpers & Brothers, of New York and London.

Fame had been circling around. Now it swooped down on her! In 1935, she was appointed Poet Laureate of Texas by the State Senate. Three years later, she was named American Mother of the Year, Honor Poet of the Year by the New York Poetry Center, and was selected as one of the ten outstanding women of America by American Publications. Two years later, she was honored with a D.Litt. degree from Baylor University, Texas' biggest Baptist seat of learning.

"All of which," whispered Grace, in one of her spontaneous, sincere asides, "I feel as if I do not deserve at all."

As American Mother of the Year, the little girl of the pewter teapot made her first trip to the great city of New York, where ceremonies, radio interviews, teas, luncheons and a reception by Mayor La Guardia awaited her. She was now sixty, her hair scarcely touched

with gray, a dimple in her cheek, and big brown eyes
that glowed with a surprised happiness.

"I'm just not one bit sophisticated," she told the
reporters, and spoke gently of her three sons, and confided that some of the two thousand poems she had
then published, had been written with one hand on
the pen and the other on the baby.

Norman was at her elbow, ever watchful, a deep
concern under his clowning. "I only hope," he wrote to
a friend, "my girl doesn't break under all this excite-
ment."

Yes, Grace Noll Crowell had achieved fame—but
not fortune. It costs money to educate three sons. Constant moving and doctor's bills do things to anyone's
budget. But, then, wealth might have been too expensive for her. Hear what she thinks about it:

> Sometimes I am glad I am not rich—
> Is it a singular thing to say?
> If I were, I should have missed
> The beautiful joy that was mine today—
> Simply because one scarlet bloom
> Came to brighten my little room.
>
> And it is strange, but when I am tired,
> A flowered plate, a quaint, gay cup,
> Or a new pan placed on my kitchen shelf,
> Can magically lift my spirit up;
> Something for a quarter—or a dollar—or a
> dime,
> That I have wanted for a long, long time.

There was nothing in Norman's Scotch ancestry to
help him understand this sympathy for the wealthy.

But hundreds of women living in modest homes the country over penned their enthusiastic agreement when she wrote:

> She who is rich may have fine things,
> But she has not waited as I have done;
> She has not gathered her treasures in
> Slowly and gladly—one by one.
> I do not think that her great rooms shine
> Any more radiantly than mine.

The gathering of those treasures, one deducts, was somewhat slow at times. For, with eager congratulations raining on her because she had just been named Poet Laureate of Texas, a radio official called to ask, "If you could have just one wish granted for Christmas, what would you ask for?"

"Spiritual or material?" queried Mrs. Crowell.

"We'll say spiritual."

"Peace," she said, without a moment's hesitation. "Peace for my mind and body. Peace of mind and body for troubled people everywhere. Peace for the world— our poor, tired, hurt old world."

"And now," said he, "supposing you ask for something material?"

And again she answered without a moment's hesitation: "A new rug for my back bedroom. This one is worn to the nap."

There was a second of surprised silence. It was not the sort of thing one expected a poet laureate to say. Then he laughed. "That's good," he said. "I'll broadcast them both." And he did.

The Crowell's present home is the embodiment of Grace's sweetest, simplest domestic poems. It is a cozy seven-room bungalow on a quiet terraced street where live—of course—the loveliest neighbors. About the home are trees, a huge magnolia in the rear, an ancient pear tree at the side.

There is not much about the little home that differs from those on each side of it, except that many of America's great and gentle have crossed its threshold; also celebrities from across the sea. But the mailman knows the difference and never ceases to marvel at the enormous amount of mail which he carries there. There are times when the poet receives literally bushels of letters! They come from all over the world—thousands upon thousands of them—and parcels of all sorts and sizes. And inside the little bungalow the ever-increasing mail is a wonder, too, to Grace. A dear delight, and as she says with swimming eyes, "the most precious pay."

I asked to see a few of these letters, and Norman produced "a few picked at random from the files." A few! They covered desks, tables, chairs, the ledges of bookshelves, the lounge, and overflowed into the bedroom, where I sorted them into compact piles along the length of the bed. Some were neat typewritten pages, other illiterate pencil scrawls. Some were written on fine, heavily embossed stationery, some on cheap notepaper. All so different, yet with one point in common —each came from the very heart of the writer.

As I dreamed and wept over them, I marveled again at that miracle I already knew something about

—the power of a pen dipped in prayer. "What a mission she has!" I mused. "This woman who so reluctantly turned from the making of bread to the making of poems!" Reverently I repeated to myself "The Poet Prays," in which she glitters even the cross upon the white altar of her life:

> The crushing of a thousand petals, Lord,
> Distills one drop of essence from a flower—
> Crush me, O God, if thereby my song makes
> Some tired heart walk with beauty for an hour.
>
> If I can bring the quick relief of tears
> To dry eyes dulled with bitterness for long—
> Gather the fragrant petals of my life
> And crush them, Lord; then help me sing my
>   song . . .

Those petals surely had been crushed, and here all around me was the fragrance of soothing and sympathy; of courage given to endure, and faith to wait.

She had called one of her tenderest, most soul-strengthening poems, "Wait." Scores of the letters I scanned that day thanked her for it. Across one she had penciled, "This almost broke my heart." It twisted mine, too:

Dear Grace Noll Crowell: Out of a dark night indeed came your poem, "Wait." It now hangs framed in my bedroom, a sort of shrine whence I may go daily to take new heart . . . to wait more patiently for my light to be lit . . . Our beloved, much-desired baby was born to us last June, handicapped by a birth injury. And we must wait during these dark days, giving him all the care we can—love and medical attention—but knowing our baby's development lies in God's hand . . .

Do you realize, then, what your words meant to me, in this dark hour I am passing through, this torture of simply waiting? . . . It has been new life to me, almost like a promise—a sign—to read this poem of yours, and I feel I must tell you of my gratitude.

A tear blotted the signature. I wondered if it were the waiting mother's or the praying poet's.

And now another, this from a dear, dutiful daughter:

I thank you from my heart's depths for "Wait." . . . For nearly seven years my little mother has been slowly slipping away, with nothing for us to do but watch and care . . . Out and away are my beloved pipe organ —and a lover—and a beautiful home nearly done— beckoning me. But here at home is my mother . . . And then, just for me it seemed, you wrote, "A heavenly lamp set on a heavenly hill, Will shine for you and point the way to go." And I am believing that "if I but wait for it, it will be lit." . . . I love you for the songs you sing.

So, too, did the radio entertainer who scribbled this note from a famous broadcasting station:

Oh, my dear, my dear, God bless you for "Wait"! God surely gave you that beautiful message to fling out to a tired, frightened, bewildered world.

I thumbed that note for several stunned seconds. Odd that one gets to thinking professional entertainers are as light as their programs!

Hundreds of the letters were from hospitals, one even from a doctor who lay critically ill in a sanitarium:

Being a physician, I think it is given to me to "look behind the scenes," as it were, and understand in what travail some of your poems were born . . . If I, too, can get something of sweetness and spiritual poise and uplift from the seemingly endless waiting for health, it will not be in vain. Thank God for you . . . and your "Wait." . . . Pray for me.

The poet prays! Poem after poem in her published books is about prayer. She prays on thresholds, at the sight of little homes on little streets, over broken-winged robins—and when she plants a rose! Perhaps her "Prayer for Courage" has been clutched to the heart of more sufferers than any other. Read this from lonely New York:

Here in this great hospital where I am living in much pain and for an indefinite time, I sleep with your brave little poem under my pillow, and read it over and over in the long night-watches. I have passed it on to the other patients here, and it has helped so many to see light instead of darkness . . . God let you go on singing your songs for the sad and suffering.

Grace treasures one tribute which she insists holds more poetry than anything she has ever written. It came from an Indian who had once been a tribal chief. He wrote:

Dear Mrs. Crowell, Your poem, "A Prayer for Courage," is the first thing that has melted the frost on the hinges of my heart, and let me weep, since my mother died.

And here is a letter from a well-known author who has found "A Pilgrim Prays" reprinted in the *Literary Digest*, and had clipped it out to keep in his copy of Marcus Aurelius. He has written from Nice, France, to tell Grace about it:

I am an agnostic, but your very sincerity and simplicity compels me to believe that "there is something far more interfused." What, I cannot say. I do not know. But there it is! . . . Not as a writer, but as one human being to another, let me thank you for the peace your little poem has given me.

From agnostic to foreign missionary is a long jump, but a Grace Noll Crowell poem easily makes it. The letter was written on board the *Asama*, bound for Shanghai, China.

I am just a plain little missionary going out again to my beloved Orientals . . . You and I are not strangers! I have known you such a long, long time through your poems. You have helped me climb many a steep hill, and yesterday when I came on board a number of steamer letters contained your lovely poems . . . Oh, how I wish I could write such poetry! May the good Lord continue to greatly bless you in your ministry to millions!

Not only letters! Oh, the parcels she receives! All containing some small, loving gift for "something priceless" the senders have found in one of her poems. A few wheels of tatting from a pensioner in Wales; a bit of fine carving from Oberammergau; kettle-holders from a lonely ranch in Australia; a quilt lovingly sewed by "a group of home-lovers"; a box of quaint notepaper from an English missionary in India.

"And this!" said Grace, her voice breaking. Just a battered box of wilted wild flowers gathered from the thin soil about a mountain cabin. "To thank you, lady . . ." And beside it a florist's box of gorgeous roses —a radiant species named for Grace Noll Crowell by the horticulturist who produced it, "To honor the poet who created a still more exquisite flower in her poem, 'I Planted a Rose.' "

Norman, as usual, was clowning. "And now," he intoned, "ask me to what I attribute her success. Go on; ask me!"

I agreeably complied. He had the answer all ready. "To having a husband like me," he grinned. And waited for the laugh. But none came. It seemed a perfectly good answer to me.

"That's a joke!" Norman, the humorist, protested. But I was thinking of Norman, the husband. "It's the truth," I said. And then I told him of what Grace had once said to me, "If you only knew the metal he's made of. He never, in all my suffering and times of being completely frustrated, has shown me one downcast look. I never could have gone on without him."

And for once, Norman had no clever comeback. He stood in silence, looking at Grace crying over the sad, wilted mountain flowers, fragrant with a sweet, wild gratitude. And then:

"There were three sizeable checks in this mail," he hailed her. "Ain't that sump'n?"

The little girl of the pewter teapot wasn't listening. With gentle hands she touched first one humble gift, then another—this letter, that. The love behind them "glittered" them . . . the day . . . her life . . . making this poetry business shine like silver in the sun.

Fifteen busy years of writing flew by, with a new Grace Noll Crowell book coming out every year, sometimes two. Then Grace's world crashed around her!

It was Christmas, 1953, when she had a sick son in one room, a sick husband in another. And one morning when she went wearily to see how Norman had slept that night, she found him in his last sleep.

"When I found him gone," she told me, "the shock was too great for me. I kept up a few days, then I collapsed completely and was ill for months. I was like an amputee with a right arm gone. I felt I would never write again."

But she had the memory of her last talk with Norman, the night before he died. As if he knew, he had urged her to continue her writing, assuring her of his belief in her ability to do so.

"So," she said, "I took a verse of Scripture, and made it my own. It was, 'Call upon me in the day of trouble, and I will deliver thee, and thou wilt glorify me' . . . I called. He delivered me! I was able to take up my pen again; and I began a little devotional book, 'Come See a Man,' to glorify Him. It seemingly pleased our Lord, for it went unusually well."

Grace had already written her first devotional book in 1951, while Norman was ill. Now, after his death, she devoted herself almost entirely to writing this type of deeply religious book—a combination of her uplifting poems and prose.

As her meditation books followed in yearly succession, the letters poured in again from readers in all walks of life, all testifying to the spiritual help she was bringing to them.

To date, ninety thousand grateful letters have come to the little girl who wanted to "glitter" gray things;

who wept bitterly because she could not write a poem, and who, as the ailing young mother of her baby son, Dean, prayed God to teach her how. Dean now lives near her, in Dallas, where he works for the Texas and Pacific railroad.

Grace is now in her soul-rich eighties, a fond grandmother, still prayerfully working at what Norman called "this poetry business."

In one of her early poems, written when she was in her forties, she told what she would like as "an enduring monument." Clean winds, she craved, cool clipped grass, a pine tree to mark her grave. And a little path leading there:

> Where the poor that I have known,
> And the piteous halt and blind
> May find their way to me,
> May pause by my side and say:
> "We are sorry she went away,
> We loved her, for she was kind."

The Little Professor of Piney Woods

Laurence C. Jones, a worried young Negro, sat on a pine log under a lone cedar tree in Piney Woods, in Mississippi's Black Belt. Close by, there sagged the crumbling ruin of a log cabin, roof-high in weeds, near a running spring.

Missouri-born, Northern-educated Jones was that rare misfit of fifty years ago, an "eddicated nigger" in the deep South—a "furriner" to even his own race, and to the average Southern white an upstart black who had forgotten his place in life.

Homeless, hungry, all he had to his name was the clothes he wore, a new diploma from the University of Iowa, and a dollar sixty-five in cash. He had pawned his precious watch, a surprise graduation gift from the fraternity men he had waited on at table, to help pay his fare here.

He had followed the star of his dream—to this! It looked as if he had come to a standstill. But giving up did not come easily to one whose favorite text still is,

"I, the Lord thy God, will hold thy right hand, saying unto thee, fear not; I will help thee," and whose philosophy is expressed in that plodding spiritual of slavery days, "Keep a-inchin' along—"

He had done a lot of "inchin' " since, as a lively lad, he had learned from his dad, head porter at the Pacific Hotel, St. Joseph, Missouri, a healthy respect for any job well done, however humble.

He had inched his way through grammar school— shining shoes, delivering papers, the only colored "newsy" on his route. He had inched his way through high school in Marshalltown, Iowa, working in a hotel for room and board, "swinging the front door" of a club in town for a dollar an evening. Always will he remember the emotion that swept through him when the entire white audience had burst into applause as he crossed the platform to receive his diploma—the first colored graduate from that school.

Finally, praying as he went, he had inched his way through the University of Iowa, averaging about four hours of sleep a night, laundering, scrubbing, serving, until the day when he was graduated, again the only Negro in his class.

Folks liked him—his spirit, his smile, his spunk, his skill. Friends, white and black, offered him good, well-paying jobs "with a future." He could have taught at Tuskegee, or been principal of a large Northern school for Negroes. He could have been captain of colored help in a palatial hotel. The father of a wealthy classmate offered to finance a musical career for him.

But to every tempting offer, Laurence Jones had

respectfully shaken his head. He had his dream! For God had already called this alert young Negro who one day would be known to thousands as "The Little Professor of Piney Woods," and to fellow-educators as "The Modern Moses of Mississippi's Black Belt."

Not from anything so startling as a burning bush had he heard his call, but through a simple motto, quietly quoted by his college president—*Noblesse oblige*. His botany teacher had explained what it meant— and right there and then, the spiritual foundation of the school of his dreams began to take shape. For to the tense, listening Negro, *noblesse oblige* now meant but one compelling thing. Because God had given him opportunities to get an education, he was duty-bound to pass on his hard-earned learning to the less fortunate of his race. "I wanted to help my people," he says simply.

Happy blending of his dreaming mother and practical father, Laurence Jones now spent every spare moment studying the basic educational needs of his race, getting the "know-how." By his senior year he knew what he must do.

And after traveling countless miles on foot, astride a mule, or by ox-cart, young Jones had finally found the place. It was here—in the heart of the Piney Woods, twenty-five miles south of Jackson, in a section teeming with hundreds of needy Negroes who were 80 per cent illiterate.

Now, sitting on the pine log, he faced facts. Nine months had gone in visiting cabins, churches, neighborhood meetings, traveling the hardest kind of way to reach county conventions, associations, any organization which might share his vision, help him finance his project. All to no avail.

The backwoods colored leaders had shown their suspicion of him—of his city suit, his Northern quick talk and ways, his education. They wanted none of him.

And as for the poor cabin Negroes, what had they to give? But how could he found a school on his college diploma—plus a dollar sixty-five?

Perhaps, he mourned, his advisers, both white and colored, were right in saying that this was no time to be even thinking of a new school, when the boll weevil was in their cotton, making their living leaner than ever.

As the boyish, bothered little professor sat on that historic log, sadly facing one hard fact after another—for he had his feet on the ground, for all his creative dreams—keenly aware of his worn suit and shoes, perhaps he might have listened to the cold voice of reason, had it not been for a barefooted Negro lad who hesitated in the clearing, peering at him.

Jones beckoned the boy to come and share his log. Then, with a welcoming warmth, he handed him a newspaper, part of the mail he had picked up on his way to this woodsy retreat.

After a few minutes, he glanced at the lad in the ragged overalls, sitting so silently on the other end of the log, and noticed that he was holding the paper upside down! Puzzled, the professor asked, "Aren't you going to read it?"

The lad shook his head. "Ah cain't read," he admitted.

Almost seventeen! And he couldn't read! The old longing of his mission swept through the little professor, grown thin through the rigors of his fruitless campaign . . . *Noblesse oblige.*

"Come back tomorrow—this same time," said Professor Laurence Jones, "and I'll start teaching you."

School began next morning with not one, but three half-grown Negroes sitting on the log beneath the old tree.

Jones opened that first session by singing "Praise God From Whom All Blessings Flow," followed by Bible reading and prayer. Throughout the half century of the school's life, the pattern has never changed—sacred song, usually spirituals, followed by a Scripture reading and prayer.

Before that first outdoor session was over, the class had grown to twelve—five boys and seven men. One of the latter was a young farmer who hoped he could learn to read and write before planting time in the spring. Another, William Yancy, was to prove a valuable asset to this tiny seed of what would one day be a mighty school, for not only did he have a little "book-learning," but he was a carpenter.

The class soon grew to be twenty-nine. When fall came, they rolled their logs around bonfires, to keep their teeth from chattering. All were thinly-clad and ill-nourished.

Winter was ahead. The class must find shelter or disband. There was the old wreck of a cabin which had sheltered sheep and goats. Could it be restored? William Yancy, the carpenter-student, thought it could. Who owned the old shack? Would the owner let them fix it up, to use as their winter school?

It was a blow to learn that the sheep shed, also the land, even the logs they had used, belonged to one "Uncle Ed Taylor," an ex-slave who had returned from the North with enough money to buy land—and with a heart reportedly as hard as flint.

Nobody in the community had a good word to say for mean old Uncle Ed Taylor. It would be wasting breath, they said, to ask that old skinflint for anything.

Jones found Taylor plowing his field one day, too busy to halt his mule and talk. So Jones trotted alongside, up this furrow, down that, trying desperately for a chance to ask a favor of this grim-faced old Negro.

Not until it was too dark to see did Uncle Ed unhitch his mule from the plow, and head toward his home and supper, with young Jones at his heels. Uncle Ed relented enough to ask this persistent young fellow in for a bite of supper, and when they had finished the frugal meal, condescended to listen.

Once again, the little professor poured out his story; told his dream of building a school to educate head, heart and hand of those forgotten Black Belt children who had never had a chance; how his exhausting work all summer had brought him only failure and despair; and how, finally, on a moment's impulse, he had accidentally started his school on a log on Taylor's land.

Jones fancied he saw a flicker of interest in Uncle Ed's shrewd, cold eyes. So he plunged on, painting in vivid words the sort of school he had in mind. Not a place where they would learn only reading, writing, arithmetic, but how to be better farmers and home-makers; where boys could learn a trade, how to grow corn as well as cotton, how to keep their cabins in re-pair, and, above all, how to be thrifty, so that they could one day buy the strip of land they worked.

"Going to take girls, too?" asked Uncle Ed.

Jones assured him that he would; and teach them how to raise better chickens and vegetables; how to sew and launder; how to plan, cook and serve a well-balanced meal, even with the little they had, and how to can surplus produce for the winter.

The little professor had said all this a hundred times to hundreds of colored audiences, with no apparent result. But this was different! Uncle Ed had lived North, knew another way of life. He, himself, had re-ceived a little schooling up there. Hadn't he proved its worth? Wasn't he now the most prosperous Negro in these poor hills?

His cold, hard face suddenly softened. He rose quickly and put a heavy hand on the surprised young man's shoulder.

"I'll give you that old sheep shed," he offered, "if you think you can do anything with it. And the forty acres around it, where you now teach."

Before Laurence Jones could swallow the lump in his throat, the old ex-slave added—"and fifty dollars."

That night, as the little professor trudged home in the moonlight, he let out a great whoop of joy! He now had the shack and forty acres, and the promise of the

152 LIVES THAT INSPIRE

deed for it, made out to "The Piney Woods Country
Life School." And, beside that, fifty dollars—all in
one dollar bills! Prophetic gift, had he but known it—
that unexpected windfall of one dollar bills!

Gleefully, gratefully, the pine log class attacked the
dirty hovel. They fixed the roof, put in a new floor and
a dirt-and-stick chimney. They re-chinked between the
old logs; then partitioned the cabin, so that one half
could serve as a school, the other as a home for their
teacher. Then they whitewashed it, inside and out.

Now they had a study hall, recreation room, office,
sewing room, carpenter's shop, basket-weaving shop,
printing shop, broom-making shop and chapel—all in
one! The cabin served for all, as the need arose.

But the little professor knew he must do more
inchin' along. There was to be a big church meeting in
two weeks' time. He asked permission to speak at it,
and there, standing in the pulpit, with the actual deed
to the forty acres in one hand, and the windfall of dollars in the other, he told of the ex-slave's gift.

The effect was electrifying! The young farmer who
hoped to learn to read and write by spring-planting
time, rose to pledge the impressive sum of fifteen dollars. Fired by his example, others raised their voices
to pledge what they had to offer—the loan of a pair of
gray mules and a wagon, tools, free labor, food for the
workers.

Laurence Jones thanked them with professional
dignity, told them he would call a mass meeting for the
following Saturday, to which they could bring their
donations, then hurried off to advertise the meeting to

all who would listen, black and white, in Simpson and Rankin counties.

But first he went to a Southern white neighbor for help and advice. From his first days in Piney Woods, John Webster, owner of the local sawmill, had been his friend, showing him a rare, rough kindness when the going was the hardest, and when he needed especially to watch his step in a state then seething with a politically-fermented attempt to prevent the education of all Negroes, since such education was considered a threat to White Supremacy.

Webster listened in silence as the eager young educator told of Uncle Ed's gift to the new school, of the coming mass meeting, and his need now for lumber.

Then the shrewd businessman had a question to ask. Suppose Jones did get the lumber, build the school with free labor, what then? He could get no state aid; no money for tuition from these destitute Negroes. How did he expect to finance the school?

Somehow, for all his struggles and setbacks, Laurence Jones had that faith which is the "foolishness" of real wisdom.

"I have friends in the North who will help me," he said. True, they hadn't so far, but once he had that first building up—something to show them for their contributions—they would surely help.

Webster was skeptical. "They'd better," he sniffed, "for you won't get any money out of here."

Laurence's heart sank. Was Mr. Webster, who had let him use one of his office typewriters to address all those appeals to his Northern friends, going to fail him now?

He wasn't, for all his common sense talk. "Tell you what I'll do," he said. "I'll give you ten thousand feet of lumber to start with—and all the rest you want on credit."

The little professor murmured touched thanks for that magnificent gift of lumber, but it was the offer of credit that made his heart sing. For it was only a few months ago that, at the close of one of his profitless speeches to a colored audience in the backlands, he had overheard one old Negro whisper to another, "All this Northern nigger wants is our dimes. Then he'll sneak off back to where he came from." It was sweet to be trusted — and by a white businessman who had the respect of all.

To Jones' stunned amazement, over a thousand people, colored and white, swarmed to that Saturday mass meeting. They poured in from the thickets and woods, whole families of them, some on weary feet that had trudged miles of sandy trails, some on mules, others packed in oxcarts and farm wagons.

Laurence seized this chance to tell them that the school of his dreams was not to be only a day school for children within a few miles' walking distance of it, but a boarding school to which boys and girls living even in remote settlements could come and stay a full term, working out their tuition and board, or paying part and working the rest.

As his keen glance swept that sea of dark faces, he saw the hope in his own heart shining now in their eyes. They grasped what he was trying to do—to give their "chilluns" a chance to LIVE, not just exist.

He told them it was their duty to do their share to make the dream come true. They could help to erect the new building in which such liberating education could begin. Men could bring their tools the following Monday morning. Women could bring food for the workers' mid-day meal.

It was time for the collection. He asked for donations and pledges, and they began to come in—a jug of sorghum; a bag of meal; a couple of live geese on a string harness, led up the aisle by a widow, the mother of nine uneducated children; some bills from the few well-to-do white visitors; and from the colored, dimes, nickels and a hundred and nineteen pennies!

Not much, but the start of his way of supporting the school—by gifts. It is supported that way to this day, when it requires a hundred thousand dollars a year to finance it.

Monday morning, bright and early, the men were back with their tools, ready to work. Yancy directed the crews of untrained volunteers as they swung axes, hauled lumber, worked on the foundation. At noon, true to their promise, farmers' wives hurried to the school grounds, laden with baskets of native food— corn bread, buttermilk, turnip greens, "tater" pies.

Day after day, the willing workers toiled until dusk, and then, after all the rest had trudged home, the "school staff," Jones and Yancy, worked on, often by the light of the moon or bonfires, until that joyful day when the building was practically finished.

Then came the devastating tornado. All night it roared and howled in its fury around the old log cabin where Jones and Yancy lay in their cots, praying to be spared, while forest pines and cedars crashed around them.

Calm came with the dawn. The men climbed over the trees and branches that blocked the cabin door, forced their way through the wreckage to the clearing, to take one anguished look at their precious school building.

There it stood—a crippled object, lifted from its foundation by the fury of the gale, twisted out of shape, a deformed victim of the savage storm.

The little professor had not had an easy life, but never before, he says, had he known such despair. Fighting back his tears, he paced around the shattered building, tortured not only by the seeming loss of it, but by the thought of the wasted effort of his people— the sacrifices they had made from their pitifully scant resources, the long hours they had so willingly given in back-breaking labor. How could he face their despair at this bitter blow?

Next day no students came and no workers. In a funereal silence, he and Yancy began clearing the wreckage and, at day's end, read their Bibles as usual and went silently to bed, Laurence to nightmares in which he strove unsuccessfully to seat fifty students on the old log.

The following morning, strange sounds pierced his gloom—shouts, laughter, gay talk. His unbelieving eyes saw his students coming back, and in high spirits.

Dazed, he heard them exulting that no lives had been lost—all that uproar, and nobody even hurt!

He found overalled farmers surveying the wrecked school building, thankful that it wasn't "plum down," trying to figure out a way to get that lop-sided, two-story pine structure back on its foundations; and expecting him to have the answer to this tough problem, as to all others. The heart that had gone out of him suddenly came back! Soon he and his old friend, Amos Gibson, were jogging along in a mule-drawn wagon to borrow jacks from the sawmill, his despair gone, his dream back.

More weeks of toil, and then the building was ready for dedication. They christened it Taylor Hall, in honor of Uncle Ed. Jones had first wanted to name it for his white friend, John Webster. But to this expert lumber man, that crude building was an eyesore. He gave one look at it, and then suggested that the honor go to another.

But "that little old sorry building," as he afterwards described it, housed eighty-five students, and soon was humming with classes in reading and writing, sewing, cooking, and carpentering, and Piney Woods Country Life School was on its way to national fame.

When school closed that first year in May, the twenty-five-year-old Jones set forth on what was to be his regular summer's task for the rest of his busy life —raising the funds to feed, house, teach and train the ever-growing number of needy children who came swarming into his school to get their first chance in life, paying for it with the little their parents could spare—a jug of cane syrup, a sack of ground meal, a chicken, a pig, a dozen eggs.

It was not easy for him to beg—even for his needy students. It was against the grain—but it was absolutely necessary. He tells how once, during that first summer of personal soliciting, waves of nausea swept him, so soulsick was he to have to "pester" people to give.

But it was worth it all to be able to return to Piney Woods with a second-hand machine for making brooms, and several hundred dollars toward meeting the next year's operating expenses.

Somehow they managed to survive those critical early years, with occasional achievements to rejoice over. As when they were able to buy a little donkey, their first "farm animal," so they need no longer plow by hand.

Or when a generous white friend sent them a little printing press to set up in the log cabin, which was soon turning out a school paper, aptly called, *The Pine Torch*, with its revealing motto, "Give the people light —they will find the way."

Or the thrilling acquisition of their first "pianner." To Negroes, big and little, all born with a song in their souls, this was a great day! It was the gift of a poor old Negro who sold his one bale of cotton, hoarded against a still rainier day, for fifty dollars, and then joyfully spent thirty of them to buy the coveted second-hand piano.

Then came the happy summer of 1912, when Principal Jones headed North, as usual, to give his fund-raising talks, but this time on an even more important mission. He was going to meet that "bright little woman" he couldn't forget, and should she be willing, bring her back as his bride.

He had met her first while he was still a University student. He had been asked to address a missionary meeting in a Baptist church, and spoke on the needs of the Southern Negro. Grace Allen was in the audience, and when asked to do so, rose to add a few words.

As the young collegian listened to this charming, cultured woman, who had once founded a school for colored children, and saw the sparkle in her eyes, and felt the exhilaration of her enthusiasm, he knew in his heart their paths would cross again.

They were married that summer in Des Moines, and when the little professor had raised all the money he possibly could for his school—and even in his new-found happiness, he kept doggedly at it!—he brought her back to Piney Woods to share his half of the little log cabin.

A new frame building went up, as if for a wedding gift. His local white friends, John Webster, and a few others from the small town of Braxton, gave the building as a dormitory to house forty girls. There was a little lumber to spare—enough to build a small manual-training shop. Neighbors, poor in cash but rich in helpfulness, made the school two little log cabins, one to be used for broom-making classes, the other as a blacksmith's shop. The little professor was humbly proud. His school was growing!

Grace was used to seeing poverty, as part of her

social service surveys, but never before had she seen such abject need as the hordes of poorly-clad, under-nourished children swarmed in, begging to be admitted to the school. No matter how tightly they crammed them in, they could only accommodate a hundred. Yet Piney Woods, poor as it was, was the only real educational facility in an area where it was estimated there were over eleven thousand uneducated children!

"We must have more buildings!" she told her over-worked husband. "Next summer I will go with you, and help you raise the money to get them." Trained in public speaking, experienced in raising money for worthy causes, she hoped she could help.

The opening day of the school's fifth year had the surge of a backwoods revival meeting. Their "'Fessor" had married a smart little woman, who, beside talking as well as he did, could teach handicrafts, cooking and canning. This seemed to give them the assurance that the new school was permanent. It was no longer a "try"; it was a going concern, here to stay.

Their joy at this certainty could not be contained. One by one, the parents of the enrolled children rose to tell their little "'Fessor" all that his school meant to them. Finally, an old Negro arose, her voice choked with emotion, to tell how she had "gone down the knee way" to implore "de Lawd" to give her "chilluns" the blessing of "eddication,"—and now, here they were! "I tell you," she finished, to a chorus of "Amens,"— "de Lawd must be in dis place."

That night, sitting by the pine-knot fire, in the lit-tle log cabin, talking over that stirring meeting, the

little professor told Grace that the school was no longer his, but theirs. It now belonged to his people. The
time had come to get a charter from the State and set
up a regular board of trustees.

And so, on May 17, 1913, "The Piney Woods Country Life School" came into existence, legally and formally, its charter another evidence of the friendship
between the two races in that section of Mississippi, for
it was signed by three local colored men, two North-
erners, and three Southern white men!

The school's first big gift of land came from one of
the little professor's Iowa University classmates. He
and his brother knew they owned eight hundred acres
of cut-over timberland somewhere in the Piney Woods
section, and they discovered that it was right next to
the school. Could he use that land?

Could he use it! More farm! More firewood! What
a joyful send-off that was to their first Chautauqua Cir-
cuit tour to lecture about Piney Woods, and tell of the
urgent need for more buildings. Little they knew how
terribly soon this need was to be burnt into their consciousness!

Christmas, 1920, should have been a happy one for
Laurence and Grace Jones. For, through the generosity
of one of their white Northern friends, Dr. J. D. Harris,
they now could celebrate it in a home of their own.
With the students now numbering two hundred, the
Principal and his wife had been crowded out to make
room for them—first, from the log cabin to a corner in
the tornado-twisted first building; from there to a
room in the industrial arts building; from there to an

old mill house on the railroad. Here their friend had found them, and, shocked that they should be living in such inadequate quarters, had promptly made them a gift of this small, comfortable cottage. A real home, at last!

They were enjoying this rare comfort, one morning, a few days before Christmas, when their breakfast peace was shattered by the shouts of "Fire! Fire!" They rushed to the window, to see an appalling sight. The boys' dormitory was burning. Like all the other school buildings, it was made of rough, unseasoned pine. There was no fire-fighting apparatus; no adequate water supply. The two-story building was soon in smouldering ashes.

Never again, vowed the shaken little professor, would he build another such firetrap on the campus! Somehow, he must raise enough money to erect a new brick building. This, in addition to the $10,000 they must now raise each year to feed and educate the two hundred students in the school.

His shoulders slumped a little, as if under the heavier load. But he clung to his text, "I, the Lord thy God will hold thy right hand, saying unto thee, fear not; I will help thee."

The big boys shivered in borrowed tents, set up on the campus; the small ones were crowded into the teachers' quarters; the teachers were crammed into his own cottage of only five rooms.

"We cannot wait for spring," he told Grace. "We must head for the North at once. If we work harder, perhaps we could get the Dulany building up by spring."

Grace wept as she left her two little sons; but this was just one more sacrifice that must be made for the hundreds of Negro children still waiting for their chance to learn.

With the thought of that lost dormitory to goad them, the little professor and his wife threw themselves into a desperate campaign to raise enough for a new dormitory. Grace often gave four lectures a day, then snatched at minutes between sessions, to solicit at stores and offices. Never a dollar, a nickel, a dime was lost to the school for lack of her making one more effort.

Back home, every member of the school was caught up in the urgency of the crisis. The girls sometimes stayed up all night to get out *The Pine Torch*, which now had 10,000 friends on its mailing list. The boys were making bricks—thousands of them!—in hand moulds, ten bricks at a time.

Persistent effort, gruelling work. But it all spelled victory. For by commencement week, they had enough money to see them through the next school year—and there stood the completed Dulany Hall, the first permanent building—another symbol of the friendship between the races, that marks the history of the school, from its pine log start to the present day.

George W. Dulany's grandfather, away back in 1850, bought at public auction, a colored girl, named Lucinda, to be his wife's personal maid. He also bought a young colored man whom Lucinda later married.

When the slaves were freed, Lucinda and her husband preferred to stay with their "Marse Bill" and his family, to whom they were deeply attached.

The children and grandchildren loved their old black Mammy, whom they called "Aunt Lunky," and she adored them. After her husband and children died, the Dulanys were all the family she had left. When she was eighty, she made a will bequeathing her estate to Major George Dulany's son, the great-grandson of "Marse Bill," who had paid $650 for her, in the long ago.

Her estate yielded nine thousand dollars, and when Major Dulany came into possession of this legacy, he thought of Laurence Jones, and his school's need of a girls' dormitory. Aunt Lunky would have rejoiced to have her savings used in this way. Major Dulany sent a check from her estate, saying he would add to it whatever was needed to complete the building; and in 1921, Dulany Hall was dedicated as a memorial to this faithful servant, and a picture of her, Bible in hand, hangs in the hall, to remind the girls of the dignity of labor.

With that first permanent building a reality, and with fire a constant threat to the other pine wood structures, the little professor and Grace once more threw themselves into a series of strenuous campaigns to raise money not only to meet the usual operating expenses of the following year, but enough more to replace the old firetraps with new brick buildings.

It was a stupendous task! During the struggle, a wonderful idea came to Grace. Every child in Piney

Woods could not only sing, but sing in harmony. Why not take out a quartette of them, that summer, and let them sing spirituals before her talks in the North? It would be a great experience for them, seeing the big world beyond their pine-clad hills. And the children, themselves, in their shy, gentle way, could tell of the school, with a special appeal.

So began the groups of "Cotton Blossom" singers, destined to bring in thousands of dollars, year after year, to help the school which even when it had reached an enrollment of 500, had only 10 per cent of the students able to pay any tuition at all.

Grace started off on that first tour with her two sons, a twelve-year-old student to care for them while she was gone to arrange bookings for the day, and her four husky back-country boys who made up the first quartette. All in a seven-passenger second-hand car, which must also carry cooking equipment and sleeping tents for those trying times when they could find no accommodations for colored people.

They had trials and tribulations, but, finally, a great triumph! For when she and the little professor returned to Piney Woods, they had raised enough money to build a second substantial brick building, helped along by the marvelous gift of a thousand dollars from the Rotary Club of Marshalltown, Iowa, where young Laurence Jones had once inched his way through grammar school. Joyfully, they named that second building, which housed the dining room and the business office, "Goodwill Hall," in honor of the many men and women of goodwill whose donations had made it possible.

In the years immediately following, with more and more "Cotton Blossoms" on tour, new brick buildings went up, as if by magic. Soon the Iowa Building, the academic hall, was ready for use; two years later, a modern boys' dormitory; and then—last, of course!— a home for the little professor and his wife. Even this they shared with the school's many visitors, calling it the Guest House.

In 1917, Mentholatum's A. A. Hyde presented the school with an elegant, efficient house car, hailed with delight by Grace, who saw that it had everything to make possible long "Cotton Blossom" trips to parts of the country not yet visited—bunk beds, cooking facilities, space for baggage. Inspired by its possibilities as a fund-raiser, she set out on an extensive tour that lasted eighteen months.

She returned to Piney Woods, overjoyed at the success of her trip, but desperately tired. She had been exhausted before, but never so completely.

"Pneumonia," said the doctor. She rallied for a while, then slipped into a coma, and never regained consciousness. They buried her under the old cedar tree, near the little log cabin.

For fifteen years she had poured her life into the school. Now she was at rest, leaving two sons, eleven and fourteen years old, who needed her just as desperately as did her grief-stunned husband, for whom there was no rest. For now he must go out alone, several times a year, doing the work of two, to insure the survival of the school.

Somehow life went on. It had to. Students, now on

the staff as teachers, took over the direction of the "Cotton Blossom" groups, supervising them on their nation-wide tours. It was in 1941 that one such group sang in a church near the campus of Upper Iowa University, little dreaming, as they put their souls into the spiritual, "Let It Breathe On Me," that there sat in the congregation someone who was to do great things for their school.

She was a brilliant little professor of English, and as she listened to that deeply-moving spiritual, beautifully rendered by the little colored children, she found herself praying that the Lord might breathe on her.

In May, 1943, she went to Piney Woods to deliver the Commencement address, and within two weeks was back, knowing that this was where she had been called to teach; that she must give up the chairmanship of a college department, and give her best to this struggling school.

The little professor knew what an asset Dr. Zilpha Ellen E. Chandler would be as head of the academic department, but could he afford to pay the salary expected of a teacher with her experience and educational background?

"What do you want?" he asked her.

"Nothing," she replied.

Possibly he was not too surprised. Many excellent teachers, white and colored, had given their services in the past, and still do. Then he asked her, "What can you do?"

"Teach English," she told him, modestly—and soon after was doing much more! While teaching the English courses in the high school and junior college, she discovered that Piney Woods' Library consisted of a few uncatalogued books in the corner of a classroom —a clean corner, but still a corner—and decided, then and there, to begin a letter-crusade for a new library.

That was the first spring after her arrival, and in two years' time, she had raised $10,000, and the cornerstone was laid. Two years later, the $100,000 building was complete, giving the school a modern, well-lighted, air-conditioned building of which any university could well be proud.

The little professor was proud to tell the world that over eight thousand white Mississippians donated to this fine library for the colored.

That done, Dr. Chandler next raised the needed money to complete a new science building, as modern in structure and equipment as the library. A lot, surely, for one little group of "Cotton Blossoms" to spark!

The greatest day in the history of Piney Woods came on December 15, 1954, when the little professor, to his utter bewilderment, found himself on the stage in Hollywood, as the star of the TV program, "This Is Your Life."

He was on one of his endless lecture tours, this time in California, when his hosts suggested that they stop to see a "show" on their way to supper. He wondered why but, always the perfect guest, fell in with their plans for the evening. He was surprised when they were ushered to front row seats, for the place was crowded, and apparently his hosts had no tickets for the show.

When Ralph Edwards dropped the "This Is Your Life" book into his lap, and pointed to the name "Jones" on the cover, the little professor said, "It must be some other Jones."

He soon found out that it wasn't. "Why, this is the real thing," he gasped, as not only the voices of those who had shared in his dream, came to his ears, but the actual people, themselves, stepped from behind the screen to greet him as Ralph Edwards turned the pages in the book of his life.

A Marshalltown High School classmate he had not seen since his graduation in 1903; Principal Graff, who had handed him his high school diploma, and a compliment he had never forgotten; a friend of his college days, in whose Delta Tau Delta fraternity he had waited tables; Mr. and Mrs. Mahaffey who had been criticized as "nigger lovers," in the early days of the school, because of their understanding and support. Then Dr. Zilpha Chandler, who so amazed the little professor by her appearance in the Hollywood studio, that he involuntarily asked, "Who's doing your work?" to the huge delight of the audience.

Then came Major George W. Dulany, Jr., who told how he had wanted old Aunt Lunky's legacy to go to a school where Mississippi girls might learn to emulate the Christian virtues that endeared her to the Dulanys.

Next, a march of some graduates of Piney Woods,

typical of hundreds of others, all living useful lives. Miss Georgia Lee Myers, first girl to board at the school — an orphan who, to help pay her way, had brought an odd assortment of contributions from friends and neighbors—a pound of butter, a dime, a chicken, two bits, some eggs. And who, after graduation, and further training as a teacher, had managed to build, mainly by her own determined efforts, three rural schools for poor Negroes in the deep piney woods.

Others marched in to greet their old-time teacher. William Yancy, now a building contractor in Louisiana —the young student-carpenter who had helped to restore the old sheep shack, and then build the tornado-buffeted first school building; and the Reverend W. C. Dixon, one of the three Negro boys who had sat on that historic log under the cedar tree, to learn to read, and now a California pastor.

They were followed by later students, Bettye Mae Jack, supervisor of the Scott County school system that numbers 23 high school teachers, 28 elementary instructors, and more than 2,200 students.

Then came R. P. McGee who came to Piney Woods not knowing his alphabet, graduated a skilled carpenter, and was now head of the Vocational Department of the Yazoo City High School.

And finally, Dr. J. R. Otis, once a student at Piney Woods School and now President of Alcorn College, the only land-grant agricultural and mechanical college for Negroes in Mississippi.

It was a wonderful show. Then, at its closing, Ralph Edwards made an announcement that surprised those

taking part in the program—perhaps, even himself!—
for it had not been rehearsed. He asked the unseen
television audience if they would be willing to send
one dollar if they knew it would help a million dollar
endowment fund that Piney Woods might live on, after
the passing of Dr. Jones.

Indeed, they would! The dollars poured into the
tiny rural post office of Piney Woods. The first day,
six bags of mail, containing $21,000; the second day,
twenty-one more bags, containing $73,000; and by the
end of the third day, $245,000 had come in, and a Jack-
son bank had come to the aid of the money-swamped
little post office, and to take over the thrilling task of
checking the cash.

Soon it had reached the $600,000 mark; then $776,-
000! Not all were dollar bills. A few grateful graduates
of Piney Woods sent checks for $100. The Brooklyn
Dodgers sent $500. The largest gift was a check for
$1,737.00, representing a dollar from each employee
of The Davey Tree Surgeons Organization of Ohio.
The smallest was from a little girl who sent a nickel, all
the money she had.

In an impressive ceremony on April 6, 1955, which
is supposed to be the birthday of Booker T. Washington, the sum of $700,000 was publicly accepted as a
permanent endowment to Piney Woods Country Life
School. This fund is expected to bring the school an
annual income of some $30,000, about a third of its
present operating expenses.

The little professor has inched a long way since he
started his school, the purpose of which, the charter

reads, is "to train the head, heart, and hands of colored boys and girls for a life of Christianity, character, and service."

From a log cabin, his school has grown to seventeen two-story buildings, and twelve others of one story. From a class of three, learning to read, to an enrollment of 500, many in high school and junior college. From a thin crop of corn, cowpeas, and collards to 350 acres under expert cultivation. Uncle Ed's 40 acres are now part of the school's 1700-acre farm. The initial capital of the school was $1.65. It is now valued at a quarter of a million dollars.

So much has changed, but not the little professor. He still returns from his trips, bringing with him some forlorn waif to be educated, often to the dismay of an already overburdened staff, but he still thinks there is room for one more.

After an exhausting day or trip, he still goes to the old cedar tree, to stand silently by Grace's grave. His hair is gray now, and there are tired lines in his kind face. The endowment fund has not yet reached the million dollar mark, so he continues to inch along, praying and working, as of old.

And he continues to dream! Of a "churchly little chapel," with chimes; of a hospital, with doctor, dentist, and nurse; of an Alumni Building, with a nook to display stories of the school's successful graduates, and pictures of their homes and families.

Some day he will rest beside Grace. His epitaph? Surely, that has already been written in Heaven, "Inasmuch as ye have done it unto the least of these, my brethren, ye have done it unto me."

Nancy Brown and Her Acre of Friends

It was morning, but so early it seemed the dead of night. Overhead the stars still shone on the great city of Detroit, wont to sleep late on a Sunday morning.

But now lights burned in bedroom windows and everywhere the drowsy streets were stirring. Front doors opened gently as coated figures crept out. Here a solitary woman, there a group of men, or perhaps a young couple, tip-toeing, with a baby wrapped in a blanket.

A factory family, mother, father and young son, stood in the safety zone, awaiting the street car, while half a block down, a well-dressed old gentleman halted a cruising taxi. He was almost in when he caught sight of the shabby strangers down the line. "Hi, there!" he shouted. "Want to ride with me?"

He bundled them in with scant ceremony. Seconds were precious. The taxi shot forward, its driver taking his direction as a matter of course. Where else would they be going but to Belle Isle? Why else get up, after a few hours of broken sleep, and start off like this, all shivering, hungry and heavy-eyed, if it were not for Nancy Brown's Sunrise Service?

And now, as the darkness lifted, a light mist, soft as a dove's wing, brooded over the city. Cars came out of the quiet side streets into the main thoroughfare, like countless little streams joining a great river on its way to the sea. Reaching the bridge of Belle Isle the swollen tide could creep forward only by inches, bearing its human cargo, a congregation of countless numbers, to an early morning service dedicated to World Peace!

We arrived at the "Shell" at last, the great outdoor theater. But where were the bleachers that should have been moved from the ball park to accommodate Nancy's great "Family"? Then slowly it dawned on me that the bleachers were there all right, but already black with people!

Only three-thirty in the morning! Yet here was a massed multitude, sitting on hard, dew-soaked benches, feet on the wet grass, shoulders slumped as though they had sat long. Patiently, pleasantly, politely waiting.

A park attendant confided that some of them had spent the night here, huddled on these hard benches. That old lady over there, beckoning to show a vacant seat, had arrived at midnight, driving from forty miles out. By one o'clock, the front seats were filling fast. At two, folks were coming in droves. By three, they were carrying in seats from all over the Island. He ran a calculating eye, long experienced in numbering vast crowds, over the assembly.

"I bet there's fifty thousand here already," he said, "and as many more on the way."

"Why do they come?" I marveled. "Like this, I mean . . . in such a big way!"

He shrugged, with a quick smile. "Why did you come?" he countered, and hurried off to guide a crippled ex-soldier — medals glinting in the lamplight, empty sleeve flapping—to that vacant seat.

Why had I come? Standing there on ground soggy from a week's rain, and chilled to the bone, I wondered. It wasn't even Easter. After a soul-searing Holy Week, the heartbreak of Good Friday, one was so spiritually awakened, so glowing with religious fervor, it seemed a small thing to arise before dawn, and watch the glad day come in a banner of crimson and gold.

But this was just Sunday, June 9th. Why, then, had I come? For the cause of World Peace, I stoutly attested. One couldn't get so positive a thing by sleeping late and wishing for it. The real effort required to attend such a service as this at such a chilly early hour was at least something tangible to lay on that white altar.

Then native honesty asserted itself, and I admitted the truth. Like all these thousands around me who had trekked in from every part of Detroit and the surrounding country, I had come because of Nancy Brown! I was here because a woman I had never seen, but whom I admired—perhaps loved—for years, had hoped gently, in her Experience Column of the *Detroit News* that "most of her family" would be there.

And what a family! Acres of them! Beyond the seated multitude, others stood in dense masses. I stood, too. It was one of those stupendous things one had to take standing. The immensity of that vast throng, amenable to one little woman's wish, following where she led! How wonderful that she always led along the Friendly Road, where understanding is, tolerance, forgiveness and good will. The road leading to Peace.

Who was this Nancy Brown? To one hundred thousand of her devoted followers, she was the First Lady of Detroit! For years, she had conducted the Experience Column of the *Detroit News*. Readers wrote letters to her, signed by a pen-name of their own choosing, and these letters, with Nancy's replies, appeared in her daily column, which rapidly outgrew its allotted space.

Her page was called "Column House," and those who wrote to it, "Nancy's Family." Many wrote only as some bitter experience caused them to seek comfort and counsel. For the rest of the time, they were content to remain "silent members" but reading the Column as eagerly as they would a letter from home.

But others wrote regularly, in fair or foul weather, year after year. As life picked them up, carrying them to the ends of the earth, they continued to write from afar. Or they settled in the home town, and as life unfolded, they told of its ups-and-downs in their letters in the Column. These faithful ones became very real and dear to the reading public, so much a part of daily life that I have heard them prayed for at church prayer meetings with as much earnestness as if they were next door neighbors. . . . "O God, help 'Deprived' in the Experience Column. Let him feel Thy hand leading him in this, his dark hour."

Nancy's Column made absorbing reading, for it was life, throbbing with every emotion in the heart of man. Life, with its love and hope and joy. Life, with its tragedy, pathos, blasted hopes, shattered romances, wrecked fortunes, broken dreams. Here, on the same page, one found selfishness and sacrifice, generosity and greed—life as it is lived on your street.

The stories of Nancy's Family went far beyond Column House. Novelists, playwrights, writers of short stories, radio scripts, and scenarios wrote asking permission to use the graphic real life material printed in its columns. Ministers preached sermons using Column letters as their texts. Bible classes built discussions around their practical problems. Some of the letters were literary gems, done by scholars tied to drudging tasks and seeking release in writing. These were frequently used in class work by teachers of English.

Thus Experience was no ordinary lovelorn column, petty and self-centered. It was given to doing things in a big way, its horizons ever widening.

One of its first projects was in the reforestation of the denuded and burnt-over areas of Northern Michigan. That was when the Column Family gave Nancy Brown a five-hundred-and-sixty acre forest as a friendship garden!

The movement was afoot to plant forty-acre plots within the boundaries of the twelve State Forests, these pine tracts to be planted in honor of anyone the donor of one hundred dollars should name.

"Andy," a Column favorite, suggested the Family plant forty acres "as a living, growing memorial to the seed of Peace," and in honor of Nancy Brown. "Wouldn't it be wonderful," he wrote, "in after years, as we drive past the tall trees, to know that the little seed of Peace had grown into a mighty forest?"

Letters and money poured in. Instead of one plot, the Family planted fourteen forty-acre tracts of cut-over forest land, all suitably inscribed, as "Andy" had wished, in honor of Nancy Brown.

The Family did everything they undertook in a big way. Years before, another Experience writer had suggested a Column Party—their first. It was decided to give it at the Detroit Institute of Arts. When the big night came, traffic was blocked for miles in that section of the city. Police estimated the crowd at one hundred thousand, but to actual knowledge thirty-five thousand Columnites attended—or tried to attend— that first Family party.

Next, it was "Doctorette" who had an idea. The pine forests of Northern Michigan, she pointed out, were so far away. Why not a remembrance near enough for all to see? Why not start an art fund for the purchase of a picture to be hung in the Art Institute as a gift from the Family, in honor of Nancy?

The nickels, dimes, quarters and dollar bills again began coming in. Art authorities named a number of eligible pictures, and these were hung where Column-ites could view them and cast their vote for their preference. In due time, the picture was purchased, and little Nancy II, all big eyes, bouquet, and perky hairribbon bow, solemnly pulled the cord that unveiled it. And to that picture was added another, and still another. Beautiful works of art bought by countless unsolicited contributions. Often it was the accompanying note that made the tiny donation look like a million dollars. As, for instance, "Am sending this money for Art Fund. And, Nancy, I did my washing two weeks to earn it. I usually send my washing out, so I feel I earned it by hard work, as I washed by hand. . . . What a lot of good we get out of the Column!"

The Family's excursion into the realm of music was at the invitation of the President of the Board of Directors of the Detroit Symphony Orchestra. Times were bad and economy budgets had no place for Symphony Concerts. The celebrated orchestra sorely needed a boost. So would Experience Column sponsor a series of concerts to be given on six consecutive Saturday evenings at Orchestra Hall? The programs would include favorite numbers selected by Column writers, and the concerts were to be especially intended for Nancy's Family.

This was an idea from outside the Column. There were Detroiters who wondered if Columnites would respond with as much enthusiasm as they showed when the idea sparked at their own hearth.

They responded! The Column went musical just as ardently as it had gone arty. Members began joyfully saving for their tickets, or earning them. The choice of suitable selections became the all-engrossing Column subject. And when they had picked their pro-

gram, music critics doffed their hats to them. Had they
not chosen as their favorite number the "Unfinished
Symphony," that flawless and ever-loved masterpiece,
Schubert's Symphony in B Minor?

Musical Detroit and Column House both profited.
Many a humble, work-weary Columnite discovered
real music for the first time—as he had discovered Art
while debating his vote for one of the ten pictures,
to be given in honor of Nancy. And Musical Detroit
discovered the warmth of a Column House audience—
and its size! "Immense!" they enthused. "Balcony sold
out hours before the concerts began. They came in
droves. Finally we were packing them in, standing up
to the fire limits. And then turning them away by the
hundreds. Quality people. They knew their music."

Column House caught compassion and kindness
from Nancy. She was always finding ways for the Family to join her in helping the poor and the suffering—
anyone in any sort of need. At first their relief fund
was made up of small free-will offerings. But it zoomed
in 1932 when it was decided, with the Column in its
fifteenth year, to bring out some of the most interesting letters in book form. Think of the tearful task—
Nancy confessed that she wept over it!—of having to
choose less than a hundred letters from over a hundred
and twenty-five thousand! But it was cheering news
to learn that Mr. W. E. Scripps, owner of the *News*,
would turn over all the profits made on the sale of the
book to the Column Family's Friendly Fund.

After that, other Column books appeared annually,
each adding money "with which to be kind" to the
Family budget. But no matter how big the fund grew,

it never was as big as Nancy's heart. Oh, the stories
the secret files could tell of homes kept together, and
lives saved! The Detroit river was cheated of many a
suicide because of Nancy's helping hand, sympathy,
counsel and sound sense.

All this was in my mind and heart as I shivered on
Belle Isle in the chill morning mist, on the edge of that
vast multitude, massed before the Shell.

A shy, friendly hand touched my arm. "Won't you
sit down?" asked a muffled knight, offering a seat he
had stayed up all night to get. I shook my head. "I can
see more, standing," I told him.

And now the men were moving about on the platform, hanging garlands of flowers, placing baskets of
roses, potted ferns. Some of the audience, stiff from
sitting, rose to offer the decorators a little advice, given
and taken with equal good nature.

"Not so much greenery, Mr. Florist! We want to
see Nancy!"

Everybody laughed. For few, indeed, had seen
Nancy Brown. No picture of her had ever been published, and press photographers who pointed cameras
directly at her never got anything but the hat, a tree
or some pillar she was hiding behind. After almost
twenty years, Nancy's elusiveness had become a leg-
end. She remained by intent, a symbol, an ideal. Con-
sequently, Columnites of all ages and nationalities, of
varied degrees of education and culture, of diverse
natures, and from every walk in life, gave her a face
and form of his own imagining, strangely like that
of his own beloved, whether of the flesh, the spirit or
his own dreams.

To one man she was a dream person, embodying all that is best and finest in womanhood; to another, the widowed mother who waited until he was graduated from the University before folding her work-worn hands together, to die in her sleep; to a third, the clever sister who would have argued him down about the New Freedom—had he ever had a sister! To men and women alike, she was an ideal, but so warmly human that she was one of their Family circle, rather than Perfection on a pedestal. So that one could rarely scan an Experience page without finding some genuine heart message, evidence of the real tie that bound this great printer's ink Family together in so close a fellowship.

It throbbed alike in the simple, "I love you, Nancy, and I like to think of you as being like my own mother," from a woman whose mother had died giving her birth; and in the cry of a young husband whose bride lay dead in their little new home . . . "She was only twenty-one . . . If I could only cry, but the tears won't come. I can't bear to enter her room—the little combs she used in her hair, and her photograph smiling at me from the mantel . . . Comfort me, Nancy. Try to convince me that life is worth living . . ."

I looked at my watch. Four o'clock and already the sky was showing a little light. With visibility, currents of curiosity swept that sea of heads. Was "Cup o' Tea" here? Nancy's one rule was that contributors to the Column must never disclose their identity. But it was exciting to guess. Surely, that queenly old lady by the rail was eighty-year-old "Gingham Grandma!" Did I know that "Blossom" was coming all the way from her Kentucky home to be here when they prayed for peace? Did I remember how she went to her little white church in the hills to pray for "Stout Fella," the young man with the sick heart? Imagine a girl, away off in Kentucky, praying for a Detroit boy who hailed from England—a boy she'd only met on the printed page of the Column!

I said I didn't remember "Stout Fella." They turned eagerly to tell me.

The heart specialist had given him just six months to live, and so he'd spent his savings on an airplane—and it was an old one, at that—and on learning to fly. If he had to die, he wrote Nancy, he was going out in style. A nose dive, and he'd be dead before he hit. Just one short stab of pain, and it would be over. He had signed his letter "Stout Fella" because that's what the doctor had called him when he took his death sentence without flinching. All he asked, by way of comfort, was a bit of a contact with Nancy—remember?—because his own mother was dead.

But he didn't die. Nancy wouldn't let him. Not on your life! She made him sell the plane. And all the Family rallied around him, and showered him with affection, advice and admonition. Then another specialist said he had a fifty-fifty chance to live, if he had the will to. And a total stranger wrote to Nancy, offering him light, interesting work, and—Oh, well, there was a lot more to that story. But, anyway, he didn't die.

"And you can take it from me," a young giant from Poland eagerly assured me, "he's here somewhere in this crowd."

A few seats away a rawboned youth, with clumsy kindness, tucked an old-fashioned patchwork quilt around the knees of a wrinkled little old lady, evidently quite deaf, for his raised voice was so loud it made us all jump.

"Cold, Mommer? It's nearly sun-up. I said it's . . . almost . . . sun-up!"

"Sh-sh-sh!" The rangy youth need not have felt so abashed, for the thousands in the ever-increasing crowd were not trying to silence him; they mere hushing themselves. A sudden lull fell on the murmur that had arisen from the bleachers like the humming of a million bees. For a group of people, the first to arrive, were seating themselves on the platform of the Shell.

"Nancy Brown!"

The effect on the crowd was one of those incredible things that defy description. It was as if a sunbeam ran along those packed benches, lighting up the faces of men and women, until that vast expanse of humanity seemed bathed in a flood of golden sunlight. It flooded through me, this intangible glowing current, electrifying my whole being. I saw it shining in the faces of those beside me, knew that they saw it in mine. A sort of spiritual sunshine, made by the friendliness, the fellowship, the good will rising from thousands of hearts. To me, it was the first sunrise of the service, significant, unforgettable. All the shadowy differences between creed and breed were lost in it. And in my heart sang the words, "Peace will be made by people, not pacts."

Twenty to five, and the sun would rise in fifteen minutes.

"There comes the program, I bet," said a man's deep voice behind me.

"Hush!" whispered his wife.

Sure enough, there at last were the cars carrying musicians and speakers. Not a minute too soon, for day was already breaking as they appeared on the platform.

All eyes were on the Shell, as Mr. W. S. Gilmore, Nancy's chief, stood to welcome her Family. They had increased in number over last year by two-and-one-half acres, he smiled. Thus, unwittingly giving the Columnites the title for their next book, "Acres of Friends," and me the title for an article about Nancy. Then he announced the theme of the meeting, "Peace," and introduced the speakers—a Jewish rabbi, a Catholic, and a Protestant minister—also a soloist, and the leader of the singing.

"The First Call" from an unseen trumpeter, and then a soaring volume of sound rose from the bleachers as thousands raised reverent voices to join in the deeply-moving hymn, "Nearer, my God, to Thee."

Across the river, Canadian church groups were assembled, hoping to hear the singing as they had the previous year . . . It came to them now, bridging the water. Softly they joined in, two God-fearing countries, linked by a hymn. Of such gossamer threads is peace wrought.

Two little wrens chirped on a nearby lamp post all through the next hymn, but they were silent, their neat little heads slanted as if to listen, while Dr. Edgar DeWitt Jones, the Column's chaplain, led the assemblage in the Lord's Prayer.

The sun was rising slowly behind the trees, and leaves sparkled with dew diamonds. Every blade of grass, every tiny stalk, every web-thread was a jeweled wonder, iridescent as if sprinkled with the dust of rainbows.

Then into this lovely world came music that matched it, Cameron McLean's beautiful voice singing "The Holy City." The crowd sat in absolute silence, scarcely seeming to breathe. A deep sigh, almost a sob, came from the stranger behind me. I knew by the lump in my own throat just how she felt. I never knew a crowd could be so still.

Then came the first address, given by Dr. Leo M. Franklin, rabbi of Temple Beth El, a distinguished scholar with a rare eloquence. He finished his moving plea for World Peace in a silence so profound I could hear a robin sing in a nearby elm.

"May this prayer be answered by that God whose glory manifests itself in sunrise and in sunset; in every blade of grass, in every budding flower; in every sound that issues from the throat of Nature's songsters—but most of all, in the hearts of men who seek and find communion with their God, and finding God, behold in every man a brother."

We all stood now to sing "Whispering Hope," and as we did so, the sun topped the trees and shone in the bluest of skies. The lights in the Shell were snapped off, being no longer needed. For here was the answer to many a Column prayer during the past dark, dismal week—a sunny Sabbath.

The birds sang with us, a Te Deum all their own,

deliriously joyful to see the sun again. As Mr. Hubert
O'Brien, representing the Catholic members of the
Family, rose to speak, a flock of sparrows took front
seats along the top of the arch. One pecked inquisi-
tively at a rose festoon. Another flew into the loud
speaker, retreating in a flurry of frightened feathers
before the resounding voice, which later, with con-
vincing earnestness told us, "The greatest challenge
to humanity today is to perfect the means of insuring
World Peace. In its last analysis, it is a matter of human faith. If the majority of people believe that peace
can be established and secured, peace will be established and secured."

The woman on my left leaned closer to whisper
solemnly in my ear, "See there! If all these fine men
believe, then we've gotta quit our doubting." I nodded
assent, although I had never doubted.

More singing. Then came the last address, so eagerly awaited, by the Column chaplain, who during a recent pilgrimage to the Holy Land, found five hundred
letters from the Family to greet him at Jerusalem.
When he invited the Column folks, once every year to
his church, so great a company were they, it took them
a month of Sundays to attend! They were divided into
groups according to the initial of their real surnames.
And even so, they filled every nook of his large church,
upstairs and down, overflowing the building.

He spoke now of the four fundamentals of life, as
emphasized by Nancy in her Column—friendliness,
forgiveness, justice and peace. And once more the marvel of it swept through me—the marvel of seventy
thousand people, many of whom had roots in a foreign

country, gathered together as a Family, on this sweet green and gold morning, in this friendly, folksy way, to think and sing and pray about World Peace.

But now the Chaplain was concluding his address: "The Prince of Peace has said, 'Blessed are the peacemakers, for they shall be called the sons of God.' May it be that each member of this vast Family, by devotion to the ideals of Peace, shall earn the right to be called a peacemaker. The time has come for a worldwide education for peace on earth, and good will among men . . . O, peacemakers, let us begin right where we are, each with himself!"

The very trees seemed to be whispering, "Peace!" as Cameron McLean's voice rose in the last solo, "How beautiful upon the mountains." A prayer by the golden-tongued Rabbi; the singing of "America," with eyes on the flag; the benediction pronounced by the Chaplain—and the Sunrise Service was over. They were already removing the flowers, distributing the roses.

Long after the benches were bare, I sat dreaming. Ghosts of bygone Column comrades came to join me. The little French war bride, married to an American soldier, and at sixteen a lonely foreigner in Detroit. Snatches of her sad depression letter, written in her "new Englerish" came to haunt me.

"Now all is gone, even hope. Noting is left. So much to give up for noting . . . So many men without work—can a cripple get work? My big boy, he keep a cross in is poket and he say God is going to feel sorry for us. Bless is heart—wish I have is faith. That to is almost gone ... O, Nancy, it is to much for me to carry. To you I come as to my mother who is no more."

And then it was the spirit of "Slim of Black Canyon" striding from the trees. A sleeve was empty. With the other arm he shielded his face. Since the war, he used to joke, that face was a pretty tough-looking affair, a tiresome mess for a girl to look at across the table three times a day.

Still he had gone to Providence where lived the lovely girl to whom he had been engaged when he enlisted. He did not see her. Her father said the Government had reported him killed in action. It seemed better to leave it that way. He had sent to Nancy a little "trinket" for Christmas, his *Croix de Guerre*. With his love. He had meant to give it to his son, if he had married and had a family, but now—

It was a little German lady who broke into my tryst with memories. She slipped in beside me, shyly offering me a piece of her coffee cake. "You eat no breakfast," she scolded. "I like you to have this. I have none to help me eat it. I live alone, my husband gone, my children."

Two sons were killed in action, she told me. They fought for the "faderland." The other was a naturalized American. He fought for this country.

"But he came back?" I asked. "He wasn't killed?"

Her quiet old hands began to shake, then her head. The shake had reached her voice when she next spoke.

"Better if he had," she shuddered. Then she touched her own forehead. "He is dead here," she choked. "They have to keep him locked up."

I sat after she had gone, jotting down notes for my story about the Sunrise Service. Suddenly I felt a light touch on my shoulder, smelled a whiff of perfume. I looked up into the face of a lovely teen-ager, fresh as this June morning. "Excuse me," she said, "but are you a Column poet?"

I almost smiled, "No." Then remembered. "Ah, that would be telling!" I parried.

She stood looking at me, her bright head on one side. "You're here under the trees, writing," she speculated.

Hastily I hid my unromantic notes. But I was immensely flattered, and probably showed it.

"Oh, you are!" she cried. "I'm sure of it!" Impulsively, she handed me her precious souvenir, a festoon rose. "Yours for friendship, forgiveness, justice and peace," she smiled. And with those sweet words ringing in my ears, I left the magic Isle for home.

It was at the 1936 Sunrise Service that a Columnite had an idea for a project so preposterous that the very thought of it should have taken away the breath of even Nancy's ambitious Family.

"Why shouldn't the Column have a carillon? Why not erect a singing tower of our own on Belle Isle, in honor of Nancy Brown, and dedicated to World Peace?"

In vain, Nancy said it was impossible; that the expense was too great; the work too strenuous; that there was no one to serve as the head. She might as well have tried to stop Niagara!

One of the Family suggested penny jars into which every Columnite could drop a penny a day—and more, if they could; and that all these homely little banks be brought to the next Sunrise Service, there to be collected and their contents poured into the carillon fund. The idea caught like wildfire. Penny jars appeared in thousands of kitchens, the city over, in factories, stores, and schools. Column House bulged with letters telling how various members of the Family were inspiring those with whom they worked to join in the campaign to give "a penny a day, to hear the bells play."

Hope soared high. Family estimates of what the penny jar collection would bring in ranged from $18,-000 and up. But all such rosy hopes were dashed to the ground when only a little over a thousand dollars was realized.

It was a terrible anti-climax. The Peace Tower and Carillon would cost $100,000, at least. It seemed to Nancy and the *News* that the only course was to give up the plan, and return what contributions were already in the fund.

This was a bitter blow to the Family whose previous projects had always succeeded far beyond anyone's expectations.

The Column went on a two weeks' vacation, to think things over. During that time, 3,000 letters flooded Column House, all begging for another chance to "carry on for the Carillon."

Some of the penny jars, they pointed out, had been delivered to the wrong place; that sudden hard shower at the Sunrise Service had prevented many from depositing their contributions in the bags provided for them at Belle Isle. Moreover, a fund started by the Column for the relief of flood sufferers had emptied many of the penny jars; and surely a sum-total of cash and pledges for ten months which showed a total of over $10,000 was not complete defeat. After all, the Carillon didn't have to be built in a year!

It seemed only fair, in view of these facts, to reconsider; and after that, to begin all over, with the Family soberly realizing that the raising of a vast sum of money to give a carillon—usually a millionaire's gift— was a colossal undertaking.

Columnites now threw themselves into all sorts of money-making enterprises — concerts, recitals, cookbooks, and their mammoth annual Christmas bazaar, which sold out, in a few hours to the last pot-holder, bringing in almost four thousand dollars!

A crippled Columnite made hundreds of leather belts; another, valuable scrapbooks; another, wonderful patchwork quilts.

Then came 1939, with Europe torn by the threat of war, and fears of its disturbing effects upon the economics of this country. The raising of more than a hundred thousand dollars for a Peace Tower now assumed the proportions of the impossible! Also the transporting of huge bronze bells across the sea could no longer be considered.

After hundreds of Column letters—some sad, some stormy—it was decided to substitute tubular chimes for bells in the Peace Tower, thus reducing the total expense of the Carillon to less than $50,000.

Detroit is a city where thousands live who have their roots in Europe, but in the war-torn years that followed, with Hitler and Stalin on the march, Columnites never wavered in making their dream of a carillon, dedicated to World Peace, a reality.

Ground was broken October 30, 1939, with Nancy handling the spade. Just a month previously Germany had invaded Poland; England had evacuated thousands of city children to the comparative safety of the countryside; and Chamberlain had made his woeful speech, "All that I had worked for, hoped for, and believed in during my public life has crashed in ruins."

The cornerstone of the Peace Tower was laid December 7, 1939, two weeks after Russia had attacked Finland. About six months later, the Nancy Brown Peace Carillon on Belle Isle was ready for dedication, its 98-foot stone tower and equipment financed by almost ten thousand Column contributors.

The Tower and Chimes were dedicated June 16, 1940, with about fifty thousand Columnites present, all aglow with joy at not only seeing their dream at last a glorious reality, but also with the thrill of actually seeing Nancy for the first time. They had heard her voice when she gave her annual radio Column talks, but never before had she spoken to them in person, or made an official appearance.

Such a little thing! So dainty and dear! So attractive, from her smart little hat to her smart little shoes! The Family gazed at their beloved Nancy, who had given them so much through the sunshine and shadow of the years; who had so enriched their lives. and from her smiling face, they gazed up at the noble Nancy Brown Peace Carillon, their love-gift to her. It was a glorious day for Column House.

The first broadcast of the Carillon chimes was on December 7, 1941, just two years after the cornerstone laying. Ironically enough, that was the day Japan attacked Pearl Harbor!

Nancy announced her retirement in January 1942, and died in 1948, in her 78th year.

I wept when I read of her death. I remembered the first time I interviewed her, as she sat, like a little queen, in a palatial office of the *Detroit News*. I remembered the many relaxing week ends I had shared with her in her cozy home, and how domesticated she had looked in a frilly apron, setting the breakfast table. I remembered the happy times we had shared when she came to Florida for a needed rest. And always she had talked of peace—World Peace, peace in Column homes.

Once I had told her bitterly, "Peace is a lost cause." It looked that way. In thirty-six days, the Nazi army had overrun the Netherlands and Belgium and captured Paris, and Britain was fighting with her back to the wall, frantically training her men with broomsticks because of a lack of guns, while Hitler was offering her his peace—as a conqueror.

"Peace!" I scoffed. "Peace is a lost cause."

Never shall I forget her quiet reply. "Nothing good is ever lost."

Nancy Brown's Peace Tower on Belle Isle stands today to remind us of that.

Sergeant York—For God and Country

Over three years it was since I last saw Alvin C.
York; and now I was on my way to visit him again.
Alvin York, the red-headed sergeant of Tennessee, who
entered World War I a conscientious objector, and
emerged an American hero, whose valor entitled him
to wear the Congressional Medal of Honor, the English Victoria Cross, the French Medaille Militaire and
Croix de Guerre, the Italian Croce de Guerra, and the
Montenegrin medal for bravery on the field.

Alvin York, the hillbilly foot soldier whom General
Pershing called "the greatest civilian soldier of the
war."

He had never intended to be a soldier. Three years
before, in his peaceful native hills, he had joined a little
church which required its members to abstain from
smoking, strong drink, and war.

Even after he was drafted in 1917, and sent to
Camp Gordon at Atlanta, his pastor kept writing him
letters, reminding him of his Christian duty to refuse
to go to war.

"My church don't believe in fighting," he told his officers.

"How do you feel about it?" they asked him. He wasn't sure. They gave him a ten-day furlough to think it over.

Back home, he found that his mother's letter to President Wilson had brought results. Official papers awaited him, releasing him from war duty. He could stay in his hills!

Poor bewildered fellow! So recently converted to a Gospel of Peace and Good Will, which taught, "Forgive your enemies; love your fellow men." And now he was drafted; and his country, which he loved, and for which his soldier-ancestors had fought, expected him not to forgive his enemies, but fight them. His claim for exemption had been refused; it was now granted . . . Christ said this; his country said that. How could he be true to both?

All through one night this soul-tortured conscientious objector knelt alone on the mountain side, praying for light . . . "Lord, I am a soul in doubt." The sun set on that lonely figure, and the stars shone down on it, hour after groping hour. The dawn of another day found him still praying, "Lord, I aim to be a good Christian, and a loyal American, too. Jes' now, they sorter seem to lead different ways. Lord, shall I go or stay?"

The dawn brightened to noon. And suddenly a sure peace flooded that seeking soul, and a swift power swept through the stiff, weary body. When the young mountaineer rose from his knees, his decision was made. He still had his scruples, but he would go. He still could not understand why Christians should wage wars. But one step at a time was enough. He'd "jes' keep on believin' in Him"—and go.

He was gone only a year and a day, but during that time the whole world thrilled to that incredible feat of his which Marshall Foch called, "the greatest thing accomplished by any private soldier of all the armies of Europe."

Just a foot soldier, the same Tennessee hillbilly who had prayed God to show him how to be a conscientious objector with a clear conscience! And now his name was headlined in the war news of Europe and America. What had he done?

On October 6, 1918, single-handed and armed only with a standard American rifle and automatic pistol, he had fought it out with a battalion of German machine-gunners over the hill his division was defending in the Argonne Forest of France.

Leading a reconnaisance team of sixteen men, York stepped beyond the edge of a thicket, to discover a German machine-gun batallion on the top of the hill. Instantly the enemy turned their guns around and opened up with a terrific attack. Ten of York's men fell, and the survivors, two of them wounded, took cover.

But not the red-headed York. The attack, he later explained, got him good and riled. He had come out ahead in many a mountain turkey shoot, taking deadly aim at each bird's head as it bobbed up from behind a log. Using the same calm, cool, precise procedure,

every time the head of an enemy gunner popped up
out of the machine-gun pit, York aimed a bullet at it.
One by one, he shot them down, until no more heads
appeared.

But the enemy was not licked. A squad of Germans
suddenly charged with fixed bayonets. York stood his
ground. Again, automatically, he employed the shoot-
ing strategy he had learned in his mountain hunting
trips. Starting with the rear attackers, he shot them
down, one after the other, until only the leader was
left. Then he shot him.

The German commander lay flat on the ground,
watching this amazing feat of hunter's skill and cool
nerve. He shouted to York that if he would cease fir-
ing, he would order his whole command to surrender.
York agreed. He had silenced 35 murderous machine-
guns, killed 25 of the enemy. Now he lined up his 132
prisoners, including the surrendering major and two
officers, and marched them back to the American lines.

Now it was York's commanding officer who could
not believe his eyes as the unperturbed mountaineer
brought in his amazing day's bag! Could it be possible?

Later he and high-ranking officers asked York to
lead them to the scene of the battle. There they found
the thirty-five big machine-guns, but, to York's dis-
appointment, not the trusty pistol he had used.

Said York, years later, "It was a higher power that
shielded me. The man on my left and the man on my
right were shot to pieces. I never got so much as a
scratch, or a cut on my uniform." He never could understand the furor his feat created. "I jes' did my
duty," he explained, "like I always aim to do."

And now I was on my way again to see this simple and truly great man. Our car was nearing the heart of the Tennessee mountains. We were already in "that-thar country where I belong," as York had so wistfully termed it when his admiring countrymen would whisk him off to their civilized cities.

Down below us snaked the white road, curve upon curve, up which we had climbed. All around rolled the great hills, like colossal ocean waves, billowing for as far as the eye could see, until they met and merged with the white caps of the sky itself. Immensity. Solitude. Timbered mountains and ravines, every tree aglow with that almost spiritual light that autumn brings to a dying foliage. Not a soul was in sight; not a cabin. All around us the everlasting hills, and the peace and power of them.

"In that-thar country where I belong." Never before had I realized how utterly this was Alvin York's country—how completely he belonged. These mountains were a part of him, a part of his very soul, his creed, his dreams for the children of their remote trails.

And, I admitted, nothing short of a world war could have pried him loose from this inaccessible section, settled and peopled by his pioneer ancestors; a rocky fastness, untouched by many of the evils of the outside world, but, at the same time, untouched by its progress. Yet he had to be pried loose if he were to get the extended horizons; the knowledge of how necessary was an education, and the vision that was to make him a leader in this section of the hills.

We were now on the famous Alvin C. York High-

way which thrills me anew every time I pass over it.
A road with a story! For after the Argonne battle, his
countrymen almost mobbed this shy young doughboy
who pin-pointed his blue eyes at them and said, "Howdy!" When he returned from France, New York went
wild over him. Ticker tape fluttered, bands played. He
was feted and entertained, with statesmen and generals doing him honor. Then he was carried on to
Washington, where both houses of Congress met him in
joint session and cheered him to the echo. He had become the popular idol, with the inevitable result. There
closed in on him scores of promoters who wanted to
exploit his fame. Vaudeville and motion picture agencies, newspaper syndicates, advertisers after his in-
dorsement. They offered him fabulous sums, enormous
advance payments. All he had to do was sign on the
dotted line.

But Alvin York shook a determined red head, and
refused. "I wouldn't betray that old uniform of mine,"
he declared, "for their thirty pieces of silver."

To go back to the road. When he finally reached
Tennessee, what a homecoming it was! Thousands of
his own folk flocked in from the far mountains. The
great ones of state and county were there to greet him.
He was Tennessee's own famous son. He could ask for
anything, they told him, and it was his. So he asked
for a road! And here it was. We were on it.

At first, just fourteen miles — which he, himself,
helped to build—from his home at Pall Mall in the
Wolf River Valley to Jamestown, the county seat. That
first link was later extended clear across Fentress
County, connecting with the main arteries of travel.

Now the children shut away in remote log cabins far back in the hills were freed. Only a few miles separated them from a good road. No longer need they plow along the muddy bed of a creek or a mountain trail to get anywhere. They could come to school—get that precious education which had been denied him, but which he was determined they should have.

But there were no good schools! The abandoned Poor House, a weather-beaten frame building, served as a makeshift classroom for a handful of pupils of high school grade. A few one- and two-roomed shacks and a single high school comprised the entire educational facilities of a county that was one of the most illiterate in the state.

With the road a reality, Alvin York now began to work for schools. He wanted them to be as modern, well-built, equipped and staffed as those in the "outland." He visualized a fine new Elementary School, and a Vocational High School, with practical courses in agriculture, home economics and manual training. "I wanted," he told me, "when I came back home, to bring my mountain folk something that would sorter last forever—that kind of a gift."

But good schools cost a heap of money. And it was up to him to raise it. But how? His first thought was of his wartime buddies. If they knew the need of these mountain children, they'd help. They were a big-hearted, square-shooting bunch, and they were used to his way of talking. For, after the Armistice, he'd been taken all over France to address moody and homesick groups of them, to "raise their morale." And they had more than listened to him. They had hung on his every word.

"It took nerve for a fellow with no education to get up and talk," he once said to me, "but I jes' done it." And now he was to do it again, and with the same success. Raised in a family of eleven children, he'd had little chance for "book larnin'." Three months of school each year for five years was all he ever had. He probably never reached the third grade.

Yet he went forth to thrill audiences of thousands with his simple eloquence; to charm them with his mountain dialect, rich in idioms brought over and handed down by those old Scotch-Irish settlers who first peopled these hills. And as he told in his simple, direct way of the need of the children back home for the education he'd never had, something inherently fine and American in the hearts of those who listened leaped out to meet the same qualities in him. The money for his mountain schools began to pour in.

It was a real effort for him to speak publicly. He was shy, and felt big and awkward and out of his element. But he plugged away, doing his honest best until he had raised, by his own efforts alone, fifteen thousand dollars; and definite plans for building the school began.

Soon he was speaking everywhere. Before legislatures, colleges, conventions; in the three largest auditoriums in New York City; to church and fraternal organizations; to Legionaires, all over the country. And whether it was to an audience of thousands in Carnegie Hall or to a half-dozen men in a committee room, he "prayed, with his hand on the handle of the door," and then did as well as he could. And God did the rest.

Finally — greatest of all miracles! — when the prophet came back to his own country, proverbially the only place where he "hath no honor," the State of Tennessee gave him fifty thousand dollars, his County matched it, and so, with one hundred and fifteen thousand dollars in the York Foundation, to build and operate schools in the mountain district, he knew that in the not-too-distant future his own mountain folk would have that gift he so wanted to bring home to them— that gift that would "sorter last forever."

Three years ago when I had interviewed Alvin York, I had sat amidst planks and mortar, under the pines, watching the imposing, ninety-thousand dollar York Agricultural Institute go up, brick by brick. Listening to plans for the big auditorium which would seat four hundred and fifty people. The countryside could talk of little else, for there wasn't a place within a radius of thirty or forty miles big enough "to hold a meetin' in." This auditorium was to have a moving-picture machine installed! There was a heap of larnin' to be had from the right sorter picture, especially for grown folks who'd never larned to read. One of them travel films, for instance. Next best thing to goin' places. . . . No, there weren't no picture places in Jamestown. Jes' as well, seein' the worthless trash some of the outland movie places showed. No dance halls, either. Mountain folks didn't believe in worldliness, nohow!

And now I was to see that school in operation— the school built on the vision and faith of a shy exdoughboy who "jes' talked," and then, church meeting style, passed the hat. Once, I remembered, it had been returned to him with four thousand dollars in its shabby crown!

We were nearing civilization. We were on the Cumberland Plateau, and within a few miles of Jamestown —only we must call it Jimtown, or the natives will know us for "outlanders."

I found it a drab little mountain town, sadly disappointing after the miles of gorgeous scenery passed to reach it. One of the oldest settlements in the state, it had gained no mellowness with the years. The courthouse in the center of the square; the hotel built on the site of the old home of Mark Twain's parents, and the two bank buildings, in one of which I found Alvin York's office—and that was about the extent of it.

It was a small office, but touched with a great and rare personality. Pictures of celebrities, most of them autographed, hung on the walls. A photograph of Lindbergh and his plane "We"; Sergeant York, between two uniformed generals . . . Stacks of crisp new copies of the first book written about York, and away off in a dark corner, a photograph of all his medals.

"All set!" announced York's brisk little secretary. "Sergeant says I'm to give you all the pictures you want, and then take you through the schools. Then to Pall Mall to see him."

"How are the schools?" I asked. He was silent, as if he were counting ten, before he answered. Then he said, "Well, of course, we need money awful bad, but the Sergeant won't compromise to get it. This week, a

tobacco company offered him five hundred dollars for
a five-minute radio talk about his war experiences—
one hundred dollars a minute, and we could use it, believe me! But the Sergeant doesn't smoke, and doesn't
believe in smoking. He said he wasn't going to sail
under any false colors, and refused the offer. That's
the Sergeant for you!"

"What's his stand on strong drink?"

"Same as always. When he was converted he gave
up drink. He went through the World War without
taking a single drink, smoking a single smoke, or cuss-
ing a single cuss. That's going some. He's that kind of a
Christian. He carries always on his person three things
—a copy of the New Testament, a copy of the United
States Constitution, and a copy of the preamble to the
Constitution of the American Legion. He's never without them. They're his life's compass."

I remembered how that Legion preamble starts
off: "For God and Country, we associate ourselves together: To uphold and defend the Constitution of the
United States of America—" Yes, I decided, if Alvin
York had a coat of arms, that certainly would be the
motto on it, "For God and Country."

I was still thinking about it as we motored out to
see the famous school which has been called, "America's Tribute to Sergeant York." In a surprisingly short
time we were there.

It is a large, handsome building, set down in a four-
hundred-acre tract of pine land. As substantial-looking
as the Sergeant himself; as serenely sure of its foundations; its two-story rows of glistening windows seeming to sparkle with the warmth of his wide smile.

Principal Brier greeted me. A tall, scholarly man, strikingly handsome, soft-spoken. We stood in the hallway, watching droves of bright-eyed boys and girls flock through the corridors to change classes. "And now," said the principal, "do come and see our auditorium."

The pride of their hearts! I stood on the stage while they showed me how the curtains worked. There was the precious moving-picture machine, spoken of with such awe three years ago! A dream come true!

"We have a short chapel service here every morning," Principal Brier told me. "A few inspiring words from the Bible. A short straight-from-the-shoulder talk. Guideposts to point the way. Then to our classes."

We visited all the classrooms, where startled eyes looked up at me with that ready-to-run glance of a squirrel. Eager, lean faces, weather-beaten, brown. Two hundred of them from the hills and valleys of Fentress and adjoining counties.

And just down the road in the big, new elementary school were four hundred other children, getting ready to graduate to all this! And all because that red-headed American doughboy had wanted to bring them back something "that would sorter last forever."

Our time was up. I climbed once more into the little roadster and away we sped to Pall Mall. We stopped long before I expected. The house before me was not at all pretentious, but a comfortable home. In the wide doorway stood the Sergeant. On the porch of the house stood Gracie, the girl he had married two weeks after returning from France, with the Governor of Tennessee officiating, two thousand people there to watch, while the Sergeant stood with his sweetheart on the rocky ridge which, before the war, had been their secret meeting place.

This was the first time I had met Grace. I noticed first her eyes—lovely, shy, of the deepest blue, they made me think of skies and stars at the same time. Her hair was the color of mountain honey. Later, I coaxed her to take out the pins and let it down. It fell to her knees.

"Howdy," said the Sergeant, and flashed his tremendous smile at me.

"Bigger than ever!" I gasped. Last time I saw him he looked like an English squire. Now he was the American farmer. All blue and tawny like the mountain sky and soil. Blue cotton cap and overalls; same pin-pointing blue eyes; same tawny mop of hair; same rosy complexion; same strong handclasp; same soft Tennessee drawl. Six-feet-two-inches and two-hundred-and-forty pounds of American manhood!

We all moved into the big living room and gathered around the log fire, and talked and talked! One by one, various members of the York clan came shyly into the fireside circle. Mother York sat near the hearth, the flickering flames touching her wrinkled face and the old hands, once so busy, now resting quietly on her knees.

I looked at the Sergeant and smiled. I wanted to ask him things, and well he knew it. "I don't want to talk about what I done in the war," he said, forthrightly.

"Of course not," I agreed. "But how about explaining your stand as a life-long teetotaler?"

There is nothing glib about him. He is a careful thinker; a slow talker. I watched him laboriously assemble his reasons, then as laboriously seek words to express them. At last he unkinked his brow.

"I've a-dedicated my life to givin' these mountain kids the right kind of education. And that kind, as I see it, teaches them righteousness as well as what they call the three R's. I heard a preacher once say that character and citizenship jes' naturally go together with good Americans. Well, I aim to make the boys and girls in my school the best Americans goin'. And liquor and that program of mine don't rightly jibe."

Always his schools! As I met those blue eyes, so troubled for fear he hadn't been able to make it clear to me, I remembered how he had once refused to run for Governor of Tennessee for fear he would be elected and have to neglect his schools for politics! Yes, the soldier who during the war had found something big enough to die for, in peace had found something big enough to live for!

Yet it was because of those very schools that trouble came to him—trouble that lasted for years, and distressed his honest soul, and probably played its dark part in breaking his health.

After the York Institute was opened in 1927, the Sergeant ran it himself for almost ten years. Then when a temporary sickness made it impossible for him to serve, he turned his school over to the State, giving the property. It was a nice gift—400 acres of land, and an established school, well staffed, in a modern building valued at one hundred thousand dollars.

With the State running the Institute, and York now recovered from his illness, he could rekindle an old ambition. He had built the various schools for his country. Now he would build a school for God. A "Study-the-Bible School" on the old York home place in Pall Mall.

Again he faced the old problem. It would take a heap of money; and he didn't have it. What he had, he'd given away.

Then came his chance to make it. Warner Brothers wanted to film his life story, making the picture from the material in the three books about York that had been published.

He was determined that it should be an honest picture. He even left his hills to go and supervise it; and if there was anything he didn't like in it, out it came! He picked Gary Cooper for the pictured Sergeant York, and would not allow them to substitute a less expensive man.

The movie biography brought him new funds, most of which he donated to build the school near his own home. He also put $38,000 of his picture earnings into the new Bible School, "one of the best buildings in Tennessee."

He paid his income tax on a capital gains basis, for which the tax is figured on only 50 per cent of the profit. "I paid them half the money," the worried York explained, "and that's all I thought I owed." But the Internal Revenue Service ruled the $160,000 taxable.

The aging York now lived under the shadow of debt —a debt to the country he loved. Unable to pay, the interest piled up until his tax debt was more than his royalties.

The Tennessee mountaineer comes of a proud, independent breed. It hurts him to owe anybody anything. He likes to hold his head high, to pay his way. The blood of generations of such sturdy, honest men flowed in the old soldier's veins.

It was a Tennesseean who started the campaign to pay that crushing tax debt for Alvin York — House Speaker, Sam Rayburn. Another Tennesseean, Representative Joe L. Evins, acted as treasurer of the York tax fund, and soon was able to report that over ten thousand patriotic Americans had gladly given money "in order that the great hero may live without the worry of a federal income tax claim hanging over his head."

Thousands of the letters and checks came directly to Pall Mall, where York endorsed them. "After that," reported the postmaster, "me and Mrs. York had to do the rest. We sent the first batch to Washington in a shoe box."

When the "Help Sergeant York Committee" had received fifty thousand dollars, one-half of that sum was paid to the Internal Revenue officials who agreed to accept it in full payment of their claim. With the other half, a trust fund was set up for the old soldier. Then a second $25,000 trust fund was donated. From these he will receive about $400 monthly for life.

Now Sergeant York, in his seventies, is partially

paralyzed and almost blind. A victim of cerebral hemorrhage, heart trouble and high blood pressure, he has been bedfast for years. Still a big, heavily-built man, it seemed as if the care of him would be more than Gracie could manage. Must he leave his mountain home, and end his days cooped up in a distant hospital?

Said a Legionaire, "For this valiant, alert hero to be hospitalized in his infirmity would be a crushing indignity. Far better to give him the opportunity to continue to live at home with his beloved wife, Gracie, and near his seven children."

But how? They found a way, as the Sergeant knew they would. Through thick and thin, his Legionaire brothers have rallied around him to help.

Now, in Kalamazoo, there lived one of them, an orthopedic surgeon who had invented an ingenious Circle-electric bed so constructed that the patient could change his own position from prone to erectly-sitting, even to standing, by simply touching a button. It looked like a large, open ferris wheel, but it was a veritable fairy wand, for this unique invention of Dr. Homer H. Stryker, a past American Legion commander, would permit Sergeant York, bed-ridden invalid, to stay in his own home and not be hospitalized.

They gave him this ingenious gift at an impressive ceremony, presided over by Governor Buford Ellington and National and State Legion heads, on October 8, 1960, the 42nd anniversary of his heroic feat in the Argonne in World War I.

Is the old soldier's work done? Don't ever ask him! Don't remind him of his precious Bible school that now stands abandoned on a weedy hilltop, near the site of the log cabin where he was born.

That $40,000 building to which he contributed all but $2,000 had an average of 77 students when he was stricken. He tried for a while to run it after he was bedfast, but it proved beyond his strength. It has been closed for several years.

One of his sons, Edward—named for York's battalion commander who helped change his mind about being a conscientious objector—is a Nazarene preacher in Nashville. Perhaps he—or some Legionaire buddies, who knows?—will some day cut down the weeds and open the closed door of that abandoned Bible school, and put it into operation again, "for God and Country."

Jane Merchant: Poet of Faith

Uncle Sam first introduced me to Jane Merchant. For years, her poems came singing or sighing their way to me, clipped from a magazine and enclosed in a friend's letter with some such admiring comment as, "She could have written this one just for me."

How I envied her! Here I was, tied to a desk while Jane—as her poems, I felt, clearly showed—was footloose to climb the highest mountain, stroll in her father's fields, roam in beauty—unshackled and free as a bird.

Then came that memorable day when I learned otherwise about this talented young poetess, whose radiant faith has enriched the lives of countless readers of this country's leading magazines. It was a stunning discovery! Jane is a semi-invalid who has never walked a step!

Confined to a wheel chair when she was two, she has been bedfast since she was twelve. Moreover, she has been deaf since she was twenty-three and also suffers now from a chronic eye disorder, which must be treated three times a day. And surprisingly, for her poems bespeak a deep culture, Jane has never been able to attend any school, except as a tiny girl when she was carried in her father's arms to the Sunday school of Inskip Methodist Church in Inskip, Tennessee.

Yet this remarkably gifted girl, still in her thirties, is the author of over 1,000 published poems, the winner of the 1953-1955 poetry prize of the League of American Pen Women, and author of four Abingdon books. For this dedicated Methodist writer, life has been truly a triumph of the spirit.

As a young child, she was "the odd one" in that happy, busy family, making a lean living on a rocky farm in east Tennessee. The little girl "hiding behind a book" had suffered since birth from a baffling bone disease. Her brittle bones snapped for the least cause and refused to knit; once, merely by leaning her weight on her elbow in bed, she broke her shoulder bone. At twelve, while she was being moved from her wheel chair, she suffered such serious injuries that she has never again been able to sit up.

For years after that she had to lie flat on her back. But now she works while reclining in bed with her typewriter across her on a little bed table and converses with visitors on "magic slates," a stack of which she keeps by her bedside.

From the start, her education was a family affair. Her brother and sisters used to come home from their studies and play school with their little sister, passing on some of their learning. Jane's mother, Mrs. C. L. Merchant, also taught her handicapped daughter—but mostly the poet-to-be taught herself through reading. She learned to read when she was five; nursery rhymes fascinated her. In a short while she was reading everything she could find. Anything to exercise her mind, to help herself to an education. Today, a librarian friend describes her as "the best-educated person I ever met."

As a girl, Jane drank in the beauty of nature as her father drove her in his dairy truck along "the green and tremulous mystery" of the Willow Road and through the beautiful Tennessee countryside. In later years, these early impressions were to find voice in many of her exquisite nature poems.

Miss Merchant sees God everywhere—in a maple leaf, a spider's web, a cloud, in "pine needles that embroider space." Who could read her poem, *Psalter*, without lifting earth-bound eyes from the grind to look for a moment at the sky?

"I have learned well, in tempests and in calms,
The holy beauty of the Shepherd's psalms;
And I have often watched with prayerful eyes
While God writes psalms, with clouds, in evening
        skies."

By the time she was seventeen, Jane had been pronounced incurable. Before her stretched a life of invalidism. Her chief concern was to earn money so she could contribute her share to the family expenses. This was one of the darkest times in her life. As her hearing faded, she could no longer enjoy the radio which once had been her listening post to "the outside." But while she was fighting to adjust herself to a soundless world, a new star began to twinkle in her clouded sky.

It was an announcement of a poetry contest in *The Progressive Farmer* magazine. Jane, who even as a child had loved to write verse, decided to enter. She wrote about the farm she knew so well, her love of the land:

"... I am not alone,
In any field where the furrows run,
Ordered and eager to seek the sun
And carry the blessings of earth and air
To the need of the nations. My place is there."

Her poem received an honorable mention—and a cash award. That was all Jane needed to rekindle the fire of her ambition to write. She began revising poems she had set aside during her "dark time," when she felt her lack of formal education, of access to libraries, and of contact with other people must prevent her from writing professionally. And her poems sold to *Good Housekeeping, Saturday Evening Post, Together,* and other top magazines.

Jane's eyes shone. Now she could contribute her share to the home finances. But she was just beginning. Soon her poems, by the hundreds, began to appear in magazines and newspapers. Editors knew nothing of her handicaps. They recognized only one fact: she had talent. Increasingly, they accepted her poems, some full of understanding, some twinkling with humor.

When the facts about Jane's physical limitations became known, dozens of readers asked how she did it. Had God granted her some unique immunity to sorrow? Jane's attitude was stated best in her poem, *Answer:*

> "Full half a hundred times I've sobbed,
>   'I can't go on, I can't go on.'
> And yet full half a hundred times
> I've hushed my sobs, and gone.

> "My answer, if you ask me how,
>   May seem presumptuously odd,
> But I think that what kept keeping on
>   When I could not, was God."

Through her poems, Jane introduces her family to her readers. One was her hard-working father, who "ploughed to the day he died"—"The silent strength of the hills was his . . . and the enduring certitudes of the earth." Another is her mother, with her "green knowledge"—who, when things go amiss, wanders off to where little green things grow, that she may receive "the helpfulness of leaves, and solacings of grass." And her remembered sayings, as "There's nothing more respectable than patches." We see the power of her motherly love in two gentle lines of gratitude:

> "And when my world collapsed about my head,
>   She built it back. 'We love you, dear,' she said."

Through her poems, we meet Jane Merchant's sister, Elizabeth, who today is a registered nurse:

> "I knew I would be well—it's hard to say—
>   If I could live until you came, each day."

Young and old, the reader meets all her family—the nieces, the nephews, the one with the "morning glory" eyes; the enraptured toddler, "discovering mud"; the small nephew whose consuming interest—if not his mother's!—is in things that creep and crawl.

Some of her tenderest poems are about the beloved oldsters, as in *Grandmother's Message:*

> "Give my love to Laura,
>   Give my love to Jim."
> Wherever Gramp was going,
>   Gran sent her love by him.
>
> "Give my love to Susan,
>   Give my love to Todd."
> Last night she whispered, gently,
>   "Give my love to God."

It was a terrible blow to Jane when, after her father's death, the family had to sell the farm and move to the city. For thirty years, Jane had lived "halfway up the sky" on farms that had forever spoiled her for a smaller view. It was a heartbreaking uprooting. Yet the valiant poet sang on—this time about the birdbath in her mother's new garden, her window box, and even a stray cow.

Once the little girl Jane lay on a hill, watching the endless acres of stars above and longing to put off the moment when she must come in at last and shrink herself "to fit a room." Physically, in later years, she may have been forced to do just that—to fit a room— to lie, hour after hour, day in, day out, in her narrow bed, gazing out through her picture window at a city street. But, spiritually, the sweep of the distant mountains is still hers.

Three of her books are devotions in poetry and prayer. Part of one of her prayers in her latest book, *In Green Pastures*, reads: "We who must spend our usual days in constricted places thank thee for every liberating glimpse of large vistas and uncluttered space. Grant, Lord, that in whatever cramped routines our customary days are spent, our minds may keep wide horizons and our hearts broad sympathies."

Yes, in soul-stirring prayers and meditations, in poems as pure as psalms, Jane Merchant sings the praises of the living God. These are her sermons, her benedictions, her life. She is, in truth, the poetess of faith.

---

[1]From Saturday Evening Post; © 1950, Curtis Publishing Co.

[2]From Country Gentleman; © 1951, Curtis.

[3]From Saturday Evening Post; © 1953, Curtis.

[4]Grandmother's Message, © 1952, Curtis, reprinted by permission of Saturday Evening Post.

I Am Not Alone, © 1952, reprinted by permission of the Progressive Farmer Co. Psalter, Answer, portions of other poems reprinted by permission of Abingdon Press, publisher of Jane Merchant's books—Halfway Up the Sky. The Greatest of These. Think About These Things, and In Green Pastures.